KT-363-029

THE

COOKBOOK

EBURY
PRESS

NOTES ON RECIPES:

Where Philadelphia is stated in the ingredients list it refers to full fat Philadelphia.
Where Philadelphia Chives or Philadelphia Garlic & Herbs is stated in the ingredients
list it refers to Philadelphia Light with Chives or Philadelphia Light with Garlic & Herbs.
Recipes have only been tested with the type of Philadelphia stated in the ingredients list,
unless otherwise specified.

All spoon measures are level unless otherwise specified.
All eggs are medium unless otherwise specified.
All fresh herbs, fruit and vegetables should be washed before use.
All eggs, pork and poultry should be thoroughly cooked.
Oven temperatures are for non fan-assisted ovens so should be adjusted accordingly.

The nutrition information refers to the main ingredients listed, not for optional ingredients
or serving suggestions.
Equivalent as salt has been calculated from the sodium nutrition value for each recipe.

Published in 2008 by Ebury Press, an imprint of Ebury Publishing
Ebury Publishing is a division of the Random House Group
This edition published in 2013 for Index Books

Text © Kraft Foods 2008
Photographs © Ebury Press 2008, except the images on pages 51, 52, 55, 56, 63, 64, 111,
127, 141, 149, 151, 152, 155, 157, 166, 169, 172, 175 and 177 © Kraft Foods Australia 2002

All rights reserved. No part of this publication may be reproduced, stored in a retrieval
system, or transmitted in any form or by any means, electronic, mechanical, photocopying,
recording or otherwise, without the prior permission of the copyright owner

The Random House Group Limited Reg. No. 954009

Addresses for companies within the Random House Group can be found at
www.randomhouse.co.uk

A CIP catalogue record for this book is available from the British Library

MIX
Paper from
responsible sources
FSC® C008047

The Random House Group Limited supports The Forest Stewardship Council ® (FSC ®), the
leading international forest certification organisation. Our books carrying the FSC label are
printed on FSC ® certified paper. FSC is the only forest certification scheme endorsed by
the leading environmental organisations, including Greenpeace. Our paper procurement
policy can be found at www.randomhouse.co.uk/environment.

Design: Smith & Gilmour, London
Photography & styling: Will Heap, Adrian Lander & Rachel Jukes
Food styling: Sarah Tildesley & Linda Brushfield
Recipe research, development & testing: Emma Warner, Valerie Hemming & Wendy Strang
Editor: Jane Bamforth
Printed and bound in China by C&C Offset Printing Co., Ltd.
ISBN: 9780091922825

To buy books by your favourite authors and register for offers visit www.randomhouse.co.uk
For more Philly recipes and ideas visit www.philadelphia.co.uk

contents

introduction

A delicious slice of homemade cheesecake or a bagel topped with Philly and smoked salmon ... just a couple of the well-loved food classics for which Philadelphia is famous throughout the world.

But Philly is not just for cheesecakes or bagels. Whether you're in the mood for something fresh and simple, or something a little more luxurious, Philly is a perfect partner for all kinds of foods. It's so versatile and can be used in all sorts of dishes, savoury or sweet - from dips to desserts, from curries to carrot cake!

In this book we've brought together over 100 of our favourite recipes inspired by the cool, creamy taste of Philadelphia.

A LITTLE BIT OF CREAM CHEESE HISTORY...

The first cream cheese was made back in 1872 in New York, USA by dairy farmer William Lawrence. Eight years later A.L. Reynolds began distributing the cream cheese and adopted Philadelphia as the brand name; inspired by the city that was considered at the time to be the home of top quality food. In 1903, the Phenix Cheese Company purchased the cream cheese business from Mr Reynolds and the Philadelphia trademark. A few years later in 1928, the company merged with Kraft, bringing the brand to the UK in 1960. Kraft now sells Philadelphia in over 80 countries worldwide.

PHILLY'S COOKING SECRETS

All the recipes have been extensively tested in our Philadelphia kitchen and tasted by a team of enthusiasts until perfect results have been achieved. We've placed some handy hints and tips within the recipes to help you along the way.

We have tried to keep the majority of recipes quick and simple with ingredients you may often include in your shopping basket or have in your cupboards at home. There are always exceptions to the rule though, so we have included recipes you can take a little more time over too.

It's often better to soften Philly before use in cooking so it's easier to combine with other ingredients. To do this simply place the desired amount into a bowl, bring to room temperature and stir, or alternatively gently beat until softened.

We hope you'll be inspired by these heavenly ideas to discover the delights of cooking with Philadelphia – enjoy!

Philadelphia's little touch of creaminess can be used in any number of light meals. So why not try something different for lunch with one of these easy recipes, or add your own twist with a dollop of softened Philly in a bowl of hot soup ... lovely!

SOUPS & LIGHT LUNCHES

spicy parsnip soup

serves 4–5 / prep time 10 minutes / cook time 35 minutes

2 tbsp olive oil
2 onions, chopped
1kg parsnips, peeled and
    diced into 3cm cubes
1 tbsp curry paste
1½ litres hot good quality
    vegetable stock
100g Philadelphia Light
freshly ground black pepper
chopped flat leaf parsley,
    to garnish

HEAT the oil in a large saucepan, add the onions and cook over a moderate to high heat for 1–2 minutes until softened. Add the parsnips and cook, covered, over a low heat for 5 minutes with the lid on, to sweat the vegetables.

STIR in the curry paste and cook for a minute and then add the hot stock. Cover and simmer for 20–25 minutes until the parsnips are soft.

ADD three-quarters of the Philly to the soup and blend with a hand blender or in a liquidiser until smooth. Season to taste. Serve with the remaining Philly stirred into the soup and garnish with fresh parsley.

tip Sweating the vegetables means to cook them slowly in a covered pan until the juices start to run. This way of gently cooking vegetables adds more flavour to the soup.

Per serving: energy 243kcal, protein 6.8g, carbohydrate 31.4g, fat 10.9g, equivalent as salt 2.2g

pumpkin soup

serves 6 / prep time 10–15 minutes / cook time 25 minutes

15g butter
1 onion, finely chopped
1 clove garlic, finely chopped
750g pumpkin, peeled and
    diced into 3cm cubes
1 large carrot, cut into 2cm cubes
450ml good quality vegetable
    stock
1 tbsp white wine vinegar
1 tsp ground cinnamon
½ tsp ground nutmeg
freshly ground black pepper
2 tbsp Philadelphia Light
2 tbsp warm milk

MELT the butter in a large saucepan. Cook the onion and garlic over a gentle heat until the onion softens. Add the pumpkin, carrot, stock and 450ml hot water, then bring to the boil.

SIMMER for 15 minutes or until the vegetables are tender. Add the vinegar and spices and season to taste with black pepper.

TRANSFER the soup to a food processor and blend the soup until smooth. Return to the pan. Mix the Philly with the warm milk and swirl into the top of the soup. Serve straight away with warm crusty bread.

tip Butternut squash can be used in this recipe instead of pumpkin. Both are perfect garnished with freshly chopped sage.

Per serving: energy 78kcal, protein 2.9g, carbohydrate 7.6g, fat 4.3g, equivalent as salt 0.7g

chicken and mushroom soup

serves 6 / prep time 10 minutes / cook time 25 minutes

1 tsp olive oil
1 large leek, finely sliced
250g closed cup mushrooms,
    sliced
2 cloves garlic, finely chopped
600ml good quality chicken stock
200g chicken breast, thinly sliced
120g Philadelphia Light
freshly ground black pepper
chopped fresh chives, to garnish

HEAT the oil in a large saucepan over a medium heat. Add the leek, mushrooms and garlic. Cook for 5–6 minutes or until tender.

ADD the stock and bring to the boil. Reduce the heat, add the chicken and simmer for another 5 minutes until the chicken is cooked through.

COMBINE the Philly with a little of the soup liquid and mix until smooth. Stir the Philly mixture into the soup, season with pepper and heat through gently. Garnish with chopped chives and serve with crusty bread.

tip Once the Philly is added ensure the soup is heated through gently and not boiled or it may separate.

Per serving: energy 135 kcal, protein 17.7g, carbohydrate 2.7g, fat 5.9 g, equivalent as salt 1.0 g,

creamy bean soup

serves 6 / prep time 10 minutes / cook time 30–35 minutes

15g butter or margarine
1 red onion, thinly sliced
2 garlic cloves, crushed
600ml good quality vegetable stock
2 medium potatoes, peeled and cut
    into small pieces
1 × 420g can mixed beans, drained
200ml semi-skimmed milk
100g Philadelphia Light, softened
flat leaf parsley, roughly chopped,
    to garnish

MELT the butter in a large saucepan, add the onion and garlic and gently fry for about 5 minutes or until softened.

ADD the stock and potatoes, bring to the boil and cook for 10 minutes or until the potatoes are tender. Stir in the beans and simmer for a further 5 minutes.

STIR the milk into the Philly and then add to the soup. Continue to heat the soup gently for a few minutes until the Philly has completely melted. Serve in warmed bowls sprinkled with the fresh parsley.

tip For a smooth soup blend in a food processor or liquidiser before adding the Philly. Return to the pan and continue as above.

Per serving: energy 174kcal, protein 9.1g, carbohydrate 19.9g, fat 7.0g, equivalent as salt 1.6g

seafood chowder

serves 6–8 / prep time 20 minutes / cook time 20–25 minutes

2 medium potatoes,
    peeled and cubed
1 tsp olive oil
1 leek, finely sliced
1 garlic clove, crushed
200g white fish (e.g. 2 small
    haddock fillets), skinned
198g can sweetcorn kernels,
    drained
180g Philadelphia Extra Light,
    softened
275ml skimmed milk
2 tbsp roughly chopped fresh
    flat leaf parsley, plus extra
    to garnish
100g peeled, cooked prawns

PLACE the potatoes in a large pan, cover with cold water and bring to the boil over a medium heat. When boiling, reduce the heat and simmer for 10 minutes or until the potatoes are tender.

HEAT the oil in a non-stick pan, and sweat the leeks and garlic in the oil with the white fish placed on top, to steam, for about 5 minutes. When the fish is cooked, it should flake easily.

DRAIN the potatoes and add to the pan with the leeks, fish and remaining ingredients. Cook for 5–8 minutes, stirring occasionally over a medium heat until the Philly has melted, all the ingredients have heated through and the chowder has thickened. Garnish with a little chopped parsley, if liked.

tip If you prefer a thinner chowder simply add a little extra milk until the desired consistency is reached.

Per serving: energy 132kcal, protein 15.1g, carbohydrate 13.1g, fat 2.5g, equivalent as salt 1.2g

baked sweet potatoes

serves 2 / prep time 10 minutes / cook time 25 minutes

2 medium sweet potatoes, washed
50g Philadelphia Light, softened
2 rashers back bacon, grilled
    and chopped
4 cherry tomatoes, quartered
freshly ground black pepper
1 small bag of salad leaves

PREHEAT the oven to 200°C, gas 6. Prick the potatoes with a fork and microwave on high for 5 minutes. Transfer the potatoes to the preheated oven for a further 20 minutes until cooked through.

SCOOP out the potato with a spoon and mash with the Philly, then stir in the bacon and tomato and season with pepper. Return the mash to the potato shells.

HEAT the grill to medium. Place the potatoes under the grill until browned on top. Serve warm with the salad leaves.

tip Alternatively, mash the Philly straight into your cooked potato and top with the bacon and tomatoes.

Per serving: energy 195kcal, protein 9.6g, carbohydrate 20.9g, fat 8.5g, equivalent as salt 1.0g

garlic and herb baked mushrooms

serves 4 / prep time 5–10 minutes / cook time 15–20 minutes

4 large open field mushrooms
3–4 tsp dry white wine
100g Philadelphia Garlic
　& Herbs
few sprigs fresh thyme
freshly ground black pepper

PREHEAT the oven to 200°C, gas 6. Wipe the mushrooms with kitchen towel and remove the stalks.

STIR the white wine into the Philly and spread evenly over the cap of the mushrooms. Top each one with thyme sprigs and black pepper.

WRAP each mushroom in a square of greaseproof paper, folding the paper over at the edges to form a seal, place onto a baking tray and bake for 15–20 minutes. Serve in the paper or remove the paper and serve immediately.

tip If fresh thyme is unavailable use a little dried thyme or fresh parsley sprigs instead. Lemon juice could be used instead of the wine.

Per serving: energy 62kcal, protein 3.6g, carbohydrate 1.2g, fat 4.4g, equivalent as salt 0.2g

chicken, chive and red pepper frittata

serves 2 / prep time 5–10 minutes / cook time 10 minutes

½ tbsp olive oil
6–7 small new potatoes, cooked and diced
2 spring onions, chopped
½ red pepper, diced
½ chicken breast, cooked and diced
1–2 tbsp fresh or frozen peas
3 eggs, lightly beaten
60g Philadelphia Chives

HEAT the oil in a small frying pan. Toss in the potatoes, vegetables and chicken. Fry for 3–4 minutes, until warmed through.

POUR in the eggs. Cook for a few minutes until the base is set and lightly browned.

PREHEAT the grill to medium. Dot the Philly across the top of the frittata and pop under the grill until golden brown.

tip This is a great simple recipe for leftovers from the fridge. Try experimenting with different ingredients such as mushrooms, ham or fresh herbs for your favourite combination.

Per serving: energy 390kcal, protein 27.6g, carbohydrate 29.6g, fat 18.8g, equivalent as salt 0.8g

parma ham and asparagus with philly lemon sauce

serves 2 / prep time 5–10 minutes / cook time 8–10 minutes

100g Philadelphia Light
2–3 tbsp semi-skimmed milk
juice of ½ lemon
freshly ground black pepper
200g fine asparagus
2 thick slices of crusty
     wholemeal bread
85g Parma ham

MIX together the Philly, milk and lemon juice in a small pan.

HEAT gently, stirring frequently until the Philly has melted, do not boil. Season with black pepper to taste. Steam the asparagus until tender but still firm.

PREHEAT the grill to medium. Lightly toast the bread and grill the Parma ham until crispy. Place the toast on 2 serving plates, top with the asparagus and ham, serve with the warm sauce.

tip The lemon sauce is also lovely with griddled or barbecued chicken.

Per serving: energy 321kcal, protein 23.2g, carbohydrate 23.3g, fat 15.5g, equivalent as salt 2.7g

sweetcorn and spring onion fritters

serves 8 (makes 16 fritters) / prep time 10 minutes / cook time 15 minutes

60g plain flour
1 tsp baking powder
¼ tsp paprika
2 large eggs, separated
100g Philadelphia Chives,
    softened
2 tbsp semi-skimmed milk
198g can sweetcorn kernels,
    drained
2 spring onions, sliced thinly
2 tbsp sunflower or olive oil

MIX the flour, baking powder and paprika in a bowl. Beat the egg yolks with the Philly and add to the flour, along with the milk, sweetcorn and onions. Mix together gently until all of the flour is incorporated.

WHISK the egg whites until stiff and fold into the sweetcorn mixture.

HEAT the oil in a non-stick frying pan and drop in spoonfuls of the mixture. Cook for approximately 1 ½ minutes until bubbles appear on the surface, turn and cook on the other side for 30–40 seconds, until golden brown. Remove from the pan and keep warm whilst cooking the remaining mixture.

tip These fritters are delicious served with a mixed salad and sweet chilli sauce or red pepper chutney.

Per serving: energy 124kcal, protein 4.7g, carbohydrate 12.3g, fat 6.6g, equivalent as salt 0.2g

beef and horseradish salad

serves 4 / prep time 10 minutes / cook time 20 minutes

650g baby new potatoes,
    washed and halved
200g green beans, trimmed
2 tsp sunflower oil
550g rump steak, well trimmed
1 small bag watercress, spinach
    and rocket salad
4 ripe vine tomatoes, quartered
¼ red onion, peeled and finely
    sliced

Sauce:
120g Philadelphia Extra Light
1 tbsp hot horseradish sauce
freshly ground black pepper

COOK the potatoes in a large pan of boiling water for about 15 minutes until tender. In a medium pan boil the beans for 4–5 minutes until tender but crisp. Drain into a colander, then cool under running water. Mix the Philly, horseradish and 3 tablespoons cold water in a small bowl until smooth.

SEASON the steak. Heat the oil in a large non-stick frying pan and fry the steak over a medium-high heat for 3 minutes on each side for rare, or until done to taste. Remove from the pan, cover with foil and rest for about 5 minutes.

DRAIN the potatoes and thinly slice the steak. Divide the salad, tomatoes, beans, potatoes and steak between four plates. Spoon over the sauce. Sprinkle with the red onion, season with freshly ground black pepper and serve.

tip If you have leftovers from a roast beef dinner why not use them to make this quick salad?

Per serving: energy 357kcal, protein 36.0g, carbohydrate 34.0g, fat 10.0g, equivalent as salt 0.7g

philly niçoise

serves 2 / prep time 10 minutes / cook time 20–25 minutes

200g new potatoes
100g fresh asparagus
2 medium tuna steaks
1 tsp olive oil
50g Philadelphia Chives
3–4 tbsp semi-skimmed milk
4 medium tomatoes, quartered
50g black olives, pitted and
  halved
25g watercress

PLACE the new potatoes in a pan of water. Bring to the boil and cook until tender.

PREHEAT a griddle pan. Brush the asparagus and tuna with the oil and pop them onto the griddle for 3–4 minutes until browned, turn over and continue cooking until browned on the other side.

MELT the Philly and milk in a small saucepan over a low heat until smooth.

QUARTER the cooked new potatoes and place them on a serving plate with the tomatoes, black olives, watercress and cooked asparagus. Top with the cooked tuna and drizzle over the warm Philly dressing.

tip Tuna should ideally be eaten medium-rare, but if you prefer your tuna cooked all the way through leave it on the griddle for a few more minutes. Be careful not to overcook the fish or it will dry out.

Per serving: energy 395kcal, protein 40.3g, carbohydrate 25.8g, fat 15.3g, equivalent as salt 2.0g

mini greek salad

serves 4 / prep time 10 minutes / cook time 5 minutes

1 courgette, cut into long ribbons
    (using a cheese slice or potato
    peeler)
1 large beef tomato
50g mixed, pitted olives
100g Philadelphia Light, softened
freshly ground black pepper
basil leaves, to garnish

PREHEAT a griddle pan and brush with oil. Cook the courgette ribbons on the griddle until browned on both sides. Leave to cool.

SLICE the tomato horizontally into 6 slices and then cut each slice in half, giving 12 halves. Chop the olives and mix into the Philly.

PLACE a half tomato slice onto each plate, top with a courgette ribbon and a spoonful of olive and Philly mix. Repeat the layers and then top with a final half slice tomato. Season with freshly ground black pepper and serve with a few basil leaves as garnish.

tip To make this a more substantial dish increase the quantities and serve with warm crusty bread as a light lunch or supper.

Per serving: energy 65kcal, protein 3.0g, carbohydrate 3.0g, fat 4.5g, equivalent as salt 1.0g

smoked salmon muffins

serves 12 / prep time 15 minutes / cook time 20–25 minutes

100g unsalted butter
120g Philadelphia, softened
2 large eggs
300g self-raising flour
1 tsp baking powder
grated zest of ½ lemon
2 tbsp chopped fresh dill
75g smoked salmon, diced
freshly ground black pepper
150ml semi-skimmed milk

PREHEAT the oven to 200°C, gas 6. Line a 12 hole muffin tin with paper muffin cases.

MELT the butter and mix in a bowl with the Philly (don't worry if it curdles at this stage). Then add the eggs, mixing well.

MIX the flour, baking powder, lemon zest and dill in a separate bowl, then add to the Philly mixture with the salmon, black pepper and enough milk to make a fairly stiff dropping consistency.

FILL the paper cases generously with the mixture and bake for 20 minutes until well risen and lightly browned. Serve slightly warm.

tip Smoked salmon trimmings could be used for this recipe and you may need to add a little extra milk if the consistency is too stiff.

Per serving: energy 200kcal, protein 6.2g, carbohydrate 19.8g, fat 11.3g, equivalent as salt 0.8g

chinese chicken salad

serves 4 / prep time 15 minutes / cook time 10–12 minutes

8 mini chicken fillets
    or chicken goujons
2 tsp five spice powder
100g Philadelphia Light
50g sesame seeds

For the salad:
2 oranges
50g rocket
100g beansprouts
2 tbsp orange juice
1 tbsp olive oil
1 tbsp soy sauce

PREHEAT the grill to medium. Cut the mini fillets in half lengthways to give 16 pieces and rub with five spice powder. Spread the Philly over the chicken and roll in the sesame seeds. Grill the chicken for 10–12 minutes until cooked through and lightly browned, turning occasionally.

PREPARE the salad. Using a sharp knife remove the peel and pith of the oranges, over a bowl to catch any juice, and divide into segments. Keep any juice for the dressing.

PLACE the rocket, beansprouts and orange segments onto 4 plates and top with the cooked chicken. Mix the orange juice, oil and soy sauce together and spoon over. Serve immediately.

tip Alternatively, use chicken breasts and slice them yourself to make strips of chicken.

Per serving: energy 332kcal, protein 38.9g, carbohydrate 10.2g, fat 15.5g, equivalent as salt 1.0g

Philadelphia and bagels were made for each other – from the classic Philly and smoked salmon, to more exotic toppings, there's a heavenly combination to suit everyone. Here are our favourite tempting sandwich ideas, great for a simple snack any time.

BREADS
& BAGELS

roast vegetable ciabatta

serves 6 / prep time 5 minutes / cook time 15–20 minutes

1 red pepper, deseeded
1 yellow pepper, deseeded
1 small red onion, peeled
1 small courgette
1 tbsp olive oil
1 ciabatta loaf
180g Philadelphia Extra Light
salad leaves, to garnish

PREHEAT the oven to 200°C, gas 6. Cut the vegetables into chunks, place in a roasting tin and drizzle with a little olive oil. Roast for about 15–20 minutes, or until the vegetables start to brown round the edges.

PREHEAT the grill to high. Cut the ciabatta loaf into 12 slices and lightly toast under the hot grill.

SPREAD the ciabatta with the Philly and top with the roasted vegetables.

tip Instead of olive oil use a flavoured oil (e.g. chilli or garlic oil).

Per serving: energy 200kcal, protein 10.0g, carbohydrate 28.6g, fat 6.2g, equivalent as salt 1.0g

roast pumpkin bruschetta

serves 6 / prep time 10 minutes / cook time 25–30 minutes

1kg pumpkin or butternut squash,
    peeled and deseeded
1 tbsp olive oil
2 sprigs fresh rosemary
freshly ground black pepper
1–2 cloves garlic, finely sliced
1 ciabatta loaf or small white loaf,
    thickly sliced
180g Philadelphia Light

PREHEAT the oven to 200°C, gas 6. Cut the pumpkin into chunks. Place the chunks in a roasting tin and toss in the oil with the rosemary, season with black pepper.

BAKE for 15–20 minutes, until golden and tender. Add the garlic and cook for a further 8–10 minutes.

PREHEAT the grill to high. Lightly toast the bread slices and spread with the Philly. Top with the pumpkin mixture and serve immediately.

tip If you find peeling the pumpkin or squash difficult, try cutting it into chunks first and then cut off the skin.

Per serving: energy 221kcal, protein 8.8g, carbohydrate 31.1g, fat 7.6g, equivalent as salt 1.0g

smoked salmon bruschetta

serves 12 / prep time 5 minutes / cook time 5 minutes

½ medium cucumber, finely
  chopped
1 tbsp dill, finely chopped
120g Philadelphia Light
zest and juice of ½ lemon
1 ciabatta loaf, cut into 12 slices
125g smoked salmon, sliced
freshly ground black pepper

STIR the cucumber and dill into the Philly with the lemon zest and juice, cover and leave to stand to let the flavours develop whilst you prepare the toast.

PREHEAT the grill to high. Toast the slices of bread until lightly golden and then place a spoonful of the Philly mixture onto each toast.

TOP the Philly mixture with the slices of smoked salmon and season with black pepper.

tip If time allows, prepare the Philly mixture beforehand and pop in the fridge overnight to let the flavours fully develop.

Per serving: energy 90kcal, protein 5.8g, carbohydrate 11.8g, fat 2.5g, equivalent as salt 0.9g

tuna and olive ciabatta

serves 4 / prep time 5 minutes / cook time 8–10 minutes

1 small ciabatta loaf
120g Philadelphia Extra Light
400g can tuna in water, drained
1 tbsp black olives, pitted
  and halved
a few mixed lettuce leaves

WARM the ciabatta loaf lightly for 5 minutes in a moderate preheated oven. Cut the loaf into 4 pieces, split each chunk in half and spread the bottom halves with the Philly.

ADD the flakes of tuna, black olives and mixed lettuce leaves.

TOP with the remaining chunks of bread.

tip Alternatively, mix the Philly with the tuna and olives, spread over the ciabatta and add the lettuce leaves just before serving.

Per serving: energy 306kcal, protein 28.5g, carbohydrate 38.1g, fat 5.4g, equivalent as salt 2.2g

chicken tikka bagels

serves 4 / prep time 5 minutes / cook time 2 minutes

4 plain bagels
120g Philadelphia Light
2 tbsp mango chutney
225g cooked chicken tikka, sliced
freshly ground black pepper
a little fresh coriander, to garnish

CUT the bagels in half horizontally. Toast until lightly browned and spread each half with Philly.

SPOON the mango chutney onto the Philly and top with the slices of chicken tikka.

SEASON to taste and garnish with sprigs of fresh coriander.

tip Add a little shredded lettuce instead of the fresh coriander or choose a salad leaf mix with coriander.

Per serving: energy 347kcal, protein 25.0g, carbohydrate 50.0g, fat 6.4g, equivalent as salt 2.1g

prawn and rocket bagels

serves 4 / prep time 5 minutes / cook time 2 minutes

4 plain bagels
120g Philadelphia Light
125g cooked, peeled prawns
2 tbsp sweet chilli sauce
handful of rocket leaves

PREHEAT the grill to high. Split the bagels in half horizontally. Toast until lightly browned and spread the bottom half of the bagel with the Philly.

STIR the prawns into the sweet chilli sauce and spoon onto the Philly. Add a few rocket leaves to each bagel and top with the other bagel half.

tip Rocket leaves provide a subtle peppery flavour that complements the chilli sauce, but they can be substituted for mixed salad leaves if preferred.

Per serving: energy 308kcal, protein 16.7g, carbohydrate 51.1g, fat 5.0g, equivalent as salt 2.5g

classic smoked salmon bagels

serves 4 / prep time 5 minutes / cook time 2 minutes

4 plain or poppy seed bagels
120g Philadelphia Light, softened
75g thinly sliced smoked salmon
a few capers (optional)
juice of ½ lime
fresh dill sprigs, to garnish
freshly ground black pepper

PREHEAT the grill to high. Slice the bagels in half and lightly toast. Spread the bottom half of each bagel with Philly.

ADD some smoked salmon, a few capers if liked and squeeze over some lime juice.

FINISH with a little fresh dill and season with freshly ground black pepper.

tip Replace the smoked salmon with hot smoked salmon flakes for a more substantial filling.

Per serving: energy 265kcal, protein 14.3g, carbohydrate 41.7g, fat 5.6g, equivalent as salt 2.1g

summer fruit bagels

serves 4 / prep time 5 minutes / cook time 2 minutes

4 plain or blueberry bagels
120g Philadelphia Light
2 tbsp mixed fruit jam
375g mixed summer berries e.g.
    strawberries, raspberries and
    blueberries

PREHEAT the grill to high. Cut the bagels in half horizontally and toast until lightly browned.

SPREAD the bottom half of the bagel with the Philly and then top with the jam.

ARRANGE the summer fruits attractively over the Philly and jam. Finish with the top half of the bagels.

tip Make these bagels in autumn, with seasonal berries such as blackberries and blackcurrants.

Per serving: energy 330kcal, protein 10.6g, carbohydrate 64.8g, fat 4.9g, equivalent as salt 1.3g

banana bagels

serves 4 / prep time 5 minutes / cook time 2 minutes

4 cinnamon and raisin bagels
120g Philadelphia Light
2 tbsp lemon or orange curd
2 bananas

PREHEAT the grill to high. Cut the bagels in half horizontally and toast until lightly browned.

SPREAD the bottom half of the bagels with the Philly, then top with some lemon or orange curd.

SLICE the bananas and arrange the fruit over the Philly and fruit curd. Finish with the top half of the bagels.

tip The bananas can be sprinkled with a little lemon juice to prevent browning if you are not going to eat them immediately.

Per serving: energy 356kcal, protein 10.2g, carbohydrate 69.0g, fat 6.1g, equivalent as salt 1.3g

Philly makes a delicious dip, either on its own or blended with your favourite ingredients. Or for perfect little party nibbles, spread Philly on mini toasts or crackers and finish with a tasty topping such as sun-dried tomatoes – simple but heavenly.

PARTY
BITES

olive and tomato bites

serves 16 / prep time 1 hour / cook time 35 minutes

16 cherry tomatoes, halved
1 tbsp olive oil
1 tbsp balsamic vinegar
½ tsp sugar
90g butter
125g plain flour
100g mature Cheddar, grated
125g Philadelphia Light, softened
½ tsp cayenne pepper
16 black olives, pitted and halved
freshly ground black pepper
sprigs of thyme, to garnish

PREHEAT the oven to 160°C, gas 3. Combine the tomatoes with the oil, vinegar and sugar in a small bowl, season with pepper and mix well. Place the tomatoes in a single layer on a baking tray and bake for 20 minutes or until the tomatoes are slightly shrivelled and soft. Increase the oven temperature to 180°C, gas 4.

PLACE the butter and flour in a food processor and process until the mixture resembles breadcrumbs. Add the Cheddar cheese and process until the dough forms a ball. Wrap in clingfilm and refrigerate until firm.

ROLL out the pastry between two pieces of greaseproof paper to 7mm thickness and cut into 16 squares (roughly 5 x 5cm). Chill the pastry until firm. Place on greased baking trays and bake for 15 minutes or until crisp and golden.

COMBINE the Philly and cayenne pepper. Spread the biscuits with the Philly mixture, then top each with two tomato and two olive halves. Garnish with fresh thyme and serve.

tip Instead of making your own bases buy cheese biscuits or crackers if you're short on time.

Per serving: energy 133kcal, protein 3.5g, carbohydrate 7.9g, fat 9.9g, equivalent as salt 0.5g

cucumber rolls

serves 24 / prep time 30–40 minutes / chilling time 20 minutes

2 large cucumbers
200g Philadelphia Light, softened
2 tsp horseradish sauce
2 tsp finely chopped fresh dill
2 tsp finely chopped fresh chives
grated zest of 1 lemon
300g thinly sliced smoked salmon
    or rare roast beef
1 small red pepper, finely sliced
    into 5cm lengths or 1 punnet
    cress, trimmed to 5cm lengths
fresh dill sprigs, to garnish

SLICE along the length of the cucumbers using a vegetable peeler, to give 24 slices. Pat the slices dry on kitchen towel.

COMBINE the Philly, horseradish, herbs and zest in a small bowl. Spread 2 teaspoons over each cucumber slice (it can be slippery at first). Top the slices with the smoked salmon or beef and trim to fit.

PLACE bundles of red pepper or cress at one end of each slice. Roll up cucumber to enclose the filling. Stand upright and refrigerate until filling is firm. Garnish with dill sprigs.

tip For a special touch wrap an extra piece of salmon or beef round the cucumber roll and secure with a toothpick, then season with salt and pepper.

Per serving: energy 33kcal, protein 3.8g, carbohydrate 1.2g, fat 1.5g, equivalent as salt 0.5g

smoked trout and wasabi pastries

serves 32 / prep time 30 minutes / cook time 15 minutes

375g ready rolled puff pastry
1 tsp chilli oil
200g Philadelphia, softened
zest and juice of 1 lime
1 tsp wasabi paste
180g smoked trout fillets
freshly ground black pepper
2 tbsp finely chopped fresh mint
    or coriander, to garnish

PREHEAT the oven to 200°C, gas 6. Brush the pastry evenly with the chilli oil until coated. Prick the pastry all over with a fork. Cut into 32 squares and place on baking sheets. Bake for 15 minutes or until golden.

COMBINE the Philly, lime and wasabi until smooth.

SPREAD the cooked pastry with the wasabi cream. Top with pieces of trout, garnish with mint or coriander and season with pepper.

tip Wasabi has a distinctive, pungent flavour similar to horseradish. If you cannot find wasabi paste use wasabi powder and make it up as per the directions on the pack. Alternatively, stir in a little horseradish sauce to taste.

Per serving: energy 68kcal, protein 2.3g, carbohydrate 4.6g, fat 4.8g, equivalent as salt 0.2g

mini philly frittatas

serves 9 / prep time 10–12 minutes / cook time 20 minutes

200g Philadelphia Extra Light,
    softened
1 small red onion, finely chopped
50g baby spinach, shredded
2 tbsp plain flour
4 eggs, lightly beaten
3 sun-dried tomatoes, chopped

PREHEAT the oven to 200°C, gas 6. Lightly grease 9 holes of a muffin tin.

COMBINE the Philly, onion, spinach and flour in a large bowl. Gradually add half of the beaten eggs and combine well. Add the remaining eggs and divide the mixture between the greased muffin holes.

TOP each muffin with a few pieces of sun-dried tomato and bake for 15–20 minutes until set and golden. Leave to cool slightly before removing from the tin. Serve warm or cold.

tip The uncooked mixture is quite runny so for ease use a small jug to pour it into the tins.

Per serving: energy 90kcal, protein 6.2g, carbohydrate 6.1g, fat 4.5g, equivalent as salt 0.4g

mexican bean dip

serves 12 / prep time 15–20 minutes / cook time 5 minutes

200g Philadelphia Extra Light
2 tsp taco seasoning mix
3 soft flour tortillas
200g re-fried beans
150g fresh tomato salsa
25g lettuce, shredded (e.g.
    1 little gem lettuce)
1 red onion, thinly sliced
2 tbsp black olives, sliced
1 red pepper, sliced
1 yellow pepper, sliced
100g sugar snap peas,
    trimmed

COMBINE the Philly and taco mix. Spread onto the bottom of a serving dish and leave covered in the fridge for at least 10 minutes to let the flavours develop.

TOAST the tortillas in a dry frying pan until golden and crispy, then slice each into 8 wedges.

LAYER the re-fried beans, salsa, lettuce, onion and olives on top of the Philly. Serve the dip with the pepper slices, sugar snap peas and tortilla chips.

tip Sprinkle a little cayenne pepper over the tortillas before frying to add a bit of spiciness and colour.

Per serving: energy 82kcal, protein 4.4g, carbohydrate 12.4g, fat 1.9g, equivalent as salt 0.7g

philly feta dip

serves 10 / prep time 10 minutes / chilling time 20 minutes

200g Philadelphia Extra Light
150g reduced-fat feta, crumbled
2 tbsp lemon juice
½ red onion, finely chopped
1 tbsp mint, finely chopped
freshly ground black pepper
whole mint leaves, to garnish

To serve:
4–5 pitta breads, toasted and sliced
1 large cucumber, cut into sticks

PLACE the Philly, feta and lemon juice in a food processor and mix until smooth. Spoon into a bowl along with the onion and mint. Stir well to combine. Chill for at least 20 minutes before serving to let the flavours develop.

SPOON the mixture into a serving bowl and garnish with whole mint leaves and freshly ground black pepper.

SERVE with the toasted pitta bread and cucumber sticks.

tip If you don't have a food processor you can make a more textured dip by mashing the Philly, lemon juice and feta together with a fork.

Per serving: energy 160kcal, protein 8.4g, carbohydrate 22.9g, fat 4.5g, equivalent as salt 1.2g

beetroot dip

serves 12 / prep time 10–12 minutes / chilling time 15 minutes

150g pickled beetroot, drained
150g Philadelphia Extra Light
a few chopped fresh chives
1 tsp lemon juice and a little zest
½ cucumber, sliced into sticks,
    to serve

CHOP one beetroot finely. Combine the remainder of the beetroot in a food processor with the Philly, half the chives and lemon zest and juice.

FOLD through the reserved chopped beetroot and place in a dish. Chill in the fridge for about 15 minutes.

GARNISH with the remaining fresh chives and serve with cucumber sticks or seeded crisp bread or rice crackers.

tip For a decorative touch soften a little extra Philly and swirl through the top of the dip just before serving.

Per serving: energy 20kcal, protein 1.8g, carbohydrate 1.7g, fat 0.6g, equivalent as salt 0.2g

sweet chilli philly

serves 8 / prep time 5 minutes / cook time 8–10 minutes

200g Philadelphia Extra Light
50ml Thai sweet chilli dipping sauce
small bunch of coriander, chopped

To serve:
50g rice crackers
½ medium cucumber, cut into
    sticks
1 red pepper, cored, deseeded
    and cut into sticks

PREHEAT the oven to 180°C, gas 4. Carefully turn out the tub of Philly onto the middle of a small ovenproof serving dish.

POUR over the sweet chilli sauce and bake for 8–10 minutes, until warm.

TOP with the coriander and serve with rice crackers and vegetable sticks.

tip Sweet chilli dipping sauces can vary in heat level. Choose one to suit your taste.

Per serving: energy 77kcal, protein 4.0g, carbohydrate 11.7g, fat 1.5g, equivalent as salt 0.4g

Liven up your everyday meals with these divine Philadelphia recipes. Philly is the perfect ingredient to melt into pasta or risotto, or simply stir through mash or your favourite veg for a light but creamy twist. The ideas are endless once you've discovered the secret of cooking with Philly!

HEAVENLY DINNERS

simple philly sauce

serves 6 / prep time 5 minutes / cook time 10–12 minutes

200g Philadelphia Light
145ml semi-skimmed milk
freshly ground black pepper

SOFTEN the Philly in a small saucepan. Gradually add 3–4 tablespoons of milk, a tablespoon at a time, until it becomes softer.

HEAT the Philly mixture over a low heat and gradually add the rest of the milk a little at a time, stirring continuously. Bring the sauce to a gentle simmer, making sure it does not boil or it could separate. Season with black pepper and serve straight away.

tip For a thinner sauce consistency gradually add a little more milk. The sauce will thicken on standing. Serve this sauce with cooked pasta, or grilled chicken or fish.

Per serving: energy 60kcal, protein 3.6g, carbohydrate 2.5g, fat 3.9g, equivalent as salt 0.4g

creamy caper sauce

serves 6 / prep time 5 minutes / resting time 20–25 minutes

200g Philadelphia Chives
2 tbsp capers, roughly chopped
½ tbsp mini gherkins, finely chopped
juice of 1 small lemon

SOFTEN the Philly in a small bowl. Add the remaining ingredients.

LEAVE to chill for a minimum of 20 minutes to let the flavours develop.

REFRIGERATE until ready to serve.

tip This goes particularly well with grilled white fish, fish cakes or scampi.

Per serving: energy 64kcal, protein 2.9g, carbohydrate 1.5g, fat 5.1g, equivalent as salt 0.8g

peppercorn sauce

serves 6 / prep time 5 minutes / cook time 15 minutes

200g Philadelphia Light
145ml good quality beef stock
2 tbsp green or mixed peppercorns
½ tsp dark soft brown sugar
   (optional)

SOFTEN the Philly in a small saucepan. Gradually add 4 tablespoons of stock, a tablespoon at a time, until it becomes softer.

WARM the mixture over a low heat and gradually add the rest of the stock, stirring continuously until smooth.

CRUSH the peppercorns and add to the sauce. Continue heating for 2–3 minutes, stirring occasionally until heated through. Ensure it does not boil or it may separate. Stir in the sugar whilst heating through if required to balance the flavour.

tip The beef stock can be replaced with chicken stock if desired.

Per serving: energy 56kcal, protein 3.4g, carbohydrate 2.0g, fat 4.2g, equivalent as salt 0.8g

pesto sauce

serves 6 / prep time 5 minutes / cook time 10–12 minutes

200g Philadelphia Light
145ml semi-skimmed milk
2 tbsp green pesto
freshly ground black pepper

SOFTEN the Philly in a small saucepan. Gradually add 3–4 tablespoons of milk, a tablespoon at a time, until it becomes softer, then stir in the pesto.

HEAT the Philly mixture over a low heat and gradually add the rest of the milk a little at a time, stirring continuously. Bring the sauce to a gentle simmer, making sure it does not boil or it could separate. Season with black pepper and serve straight away.

tip For a quick supper stir the sauce into cooked penne pasta, mixed with grilled chicken pieces and cooked broccoli florets.

Per serving: energy 60kcal, protein 3.6g, carbohydrate 2.5g, fat 3.9g, equivalent as salt 0.4g

PASTA

mixed pepper and herb cannelloni

serves 2 / prep time 20 minutes / cook time 15 – 20 minutes

1 tbsp olive or sunflower oil
1 small onion, chopped
½ red pepper, sliced thinly
½ yellow pepper, sliced thinly
60g Philadelphia Garlic & Herbs
1 tbsp semi-skimmed milk
2 large sheets of fresh lasagne
400g can chopped tomatoes,
  drained
1 tsp dried mixed herbs
large handful rocket, to serve

PREHEAT the oven to 190°C, gas 5. Heat the oil in a pan and fry the onion and peppers for 3–4 minutes until softened and beginning to brown. Off the heat, stir in the Philly and milk.

FOLLOW directions on the pack to cook the lasagne (it may be necessary to soak in boiling water for 5 minutes to soften). Cut each sheet in half widthways. Heat the tomatoes with the herbs in a small pan.

PLACE a spoonful of Philly and pepper mixture at one end of each piece of lasagne and roll up into a tube. Place all 4 into a greased ovenproof dish.

TOP with the tomato mixture and bake for 15–20 minutes. Serve topped with the rocket.

tip For a quick alternative use a can of chopped tomatoes with herbs to pour straight over the filled pasta tubes before baking.

Per serving: energy 350kcal, protein 12.0g, carbohydrate 52.2g, fat 11.8g, equivalent as salt 0.6g

spaghetti carbonara

serves 4 / prep time 10 minutes / cook time 20 minutes

300g dried spaghetti
1 tbsp olive oil
1 small onion, finely sliced
1 clove garlic, crushed
120g Philadelphia Light, softened
75ml semi-skimmed milk
4 slices smoked ham, diced
15g flat leaf parsley, roughly
    chopped

COOK the spaghetti in a large saucepan of boiling water for about 8 minutes or as directed on the pack.

HEAT the oil in a frying pan and cook the onion and garlic until softened. Add the Philly and milk and continue to cook over a low heat until the Philly has melted, then stir in the ham pieces.

DRAIN the pasta and return to the saucepan with the Philly mixture and all but 1 tablespoon of the chopped parsley. Gently stir the Philly mixture through the pasta and garnish with the remaining parsley.

tip As an alternative, use pieces of cooked crispy bacon or pancetta instead of the ham.

Per serving: energy 274kcal, protein 13.3g, carbohydrate 38.5g, fat 8.5g, equivalent as salt 1.0g

creamy lemon and thyme spaghetti

serves 4 / prep time 5 minutes / cook time 15 minutes

300g dried spaghetti
120g Philadelphia Light
zest and juice of 1 lemon
1 tbsp fresh thyme, chopped
100g frozen peas
freshly ground black pepper

COOK the spaghetti in a large pan of boiling water for about 8 minutes or according to the instructions on the pack, then drain.

HEAT all of the remaining ingredients gently in a pan for 3–4 minutes until the peas are cooked.

COMBINE the sauce with the spaghetti, season with black pepper and serve.

tip This sauce has a lovely tang but if it is too sharp and lemony, add a pinch of sugar to balance the flavour.

Per serving: energy 233kcal, protein 9.9g, carbohydrate 39.6g, fat 4.9g, equivalent as salt 0.3g

bacon and tomato lasagne

serves 4 / prep time 15–20 minutes / cook time 20–25 minutes

6 sheets fresh lasagne
1 tbsp olive or sunflower oil
1 red onion, chopped
6 rashers reduced salt back
    bacon, diced
6 medium tomatoes, skinned,
    de-seeded and flesh chopped
1 tsp dried mixed herbs
60g Philadelphia Light
2 tbsp semi-skimmed milk

For the topping:
60g Philadelphia Light
2 tbsp semi-skimmed milk
25g Cheddar cheese, grated
1 tsp Dijon mustard

PREHEAT the oven to 190°C, gas 5. Follow directions on the pack to cook the lasagne (it may be necessary to soak in boiling water for 5 minutes to soften). Heat the oil in a pan and fry the onion and bacon until beginning to brown, approx 3–4 minutes.

ADD the tomatoes and herbs, reduce the heat to simmer and cook for a further 3–4 minutes. Stir in the Philly and milk off the heat.

PLACE 2 sheets of lasagne into an ovenproof dish, top with half the tomato mixture, then repeat with 2 more sheets of lasagne and the remaining tomato mixture. Finish with the remaining lasagne.

MIX together the topping ingredients and spread on top. Bake for 20 minutes or until browned.

tip To make 4 individual lasagnes cut the lasagne sheets in half and divide the mixture between 4 individual ovenproof dishes. Test after 15 minutes cooking as they may not need the full 20 minutes.

Per serving: energy 543kcal, protein 27.1g, carbohydrate 65.2g, fat 21.1g, equivalent as salt 2.0g

chicken and sunblush tomato pasta

serves 4 / prep time 5 minutes / cook time 15–20 minutes

300g dried pasta shapes
   (e.g. spirals, penne or shells)
1 tbsp olive oil
2 chicken breasts, cut into strips
120g Philadelphia Garlic & Herbs
1 tbsp semi-skimmed milk
2 tsp sundried tomato paste
50g sunblush tomatoes, chopped
1 tbsp chopped fresh flat
   leaf parsley

COOK the pasta according to instructions on the pack and drain.

HEAT the oil in a griddle pan and cook the chicken over a medium heat for about 5–8 minutes until browned and cooked through.

HEAT the Philly gently in a small pan with the milk, sundried tomato paste, sunblush tomatoes and chopped parsley. Add the cooked chicken strips and heat through. Combine with the pasta and serve straight away.

tip If you don't have a griddle pan, simply cook the chicken in a frying pan with half a tablespoon of oil.

Per serving: energy 471kcal, protein 31.2g, carbohydrate 56.8g, fat 13.4g, equivalent as salt 0.5g

fettucine with spicy tomato and courgettes

serves 4 / prep time 10–12 minutes / cook time 10–12 minutes

300g dried fettucine or tagliatelle
1 tbsp olive oil
½ red chilli, finely chopped and
    deseeded
2 medium courgettes, thinly sliced
3 medium tomatoes, skinned,
    chopped and deseeded
120g Philadelphia Light
2 tbsp semi-skimmed milk
freshly ground black pepper

COOK the pasta according to instructions on the pack and drain.

HEAT the oil in a large saucepan, add the chilli and courgettes and cook over a medium to high heat for 3–4 minutes.

REDUCE the heat, add the tomatoes, Philly and milk and cook for 2–3 minutes without boiling, season to taste. Combine with the pasta and serve.

tip Plunge the tomatoes in boiling water to help loosen the skins.

Per serving: energy 261kcal, protein 9.8g, carbohydrate 40.0g, fat 7.8g, equivalent as salt 0.3g

smoked salmon tagliatelle

serves 2 / prep time 10 minutes / cook time 10–15 minutes

½ tbsp olive oil
2 spring onions, finely sliced
100g Philadelphia Garlic & Herbs
3–4 tbsp semi-skimmed milk
zest and juice of ½ lemon
250g fresh tagliatelle verde
125g smoked salmon, sliced
   into strips
a few chopped fresh herbs,
   to garnish
freshly ground black pepper

HEAT the oil in a small pan and gently fry the onions until softened. Add the Philly, milk and lemon juice, stirring over a low heat until melted.

ADD the pasta to a large pan of boiling water and cook as directed on the pack. Drain and place back in the pan. Carefully stir in the Philly sauce and smoked salmon strips.

GARNISH with the lemon zest and fresh herbs and season with black pepper.

tip Serve this creamy pasta dish with steamed asparagus tips or mange tout.

Per serving: energy 561kcal, protein 34.8g, carbohydrate 72.7g, fat 16.8g, equivalent as salt 3.5g

chicken and olive penne

serves 2 / prep time 10–12 minutes / cook time 10–15 minutes

1 tbsp olive oil
2 chicken breasts, cut into pieces
½ sprig fresh rosemary, chopped
½ tbsp grated Parmesan cheese
250g fresh penne pasta
½ red pepper, finely diced
½ tbsp chopped fresh flat
    leaf parsley
100g Philadelphia Light
4–5 tbsp semi-skimmed milk
1 tbsp black or green olives, sliced
freshly ground black pepper

HEAT half the oil in a large pan and fry the chicken until golden brown. Add the rosemary, Parmesan and season with black pepper and continue cooking over a medium heat until the chicken is thoroughly cooked.

PLACE the pasta in a large pan of boiling water and cook as directed on the pack. Drain.

FRY the red pepper gently in the remaining oil, add the parsley, Philly and milk. Stir until melted then add the drained pasta, olives and chicken.

tip Serve this tasty pasta dish with a basil and tomato salad for a simple midweek supper.

Per serving: energy 717kcal, protein 62.5g, carbohydrate 75.7g, fat 20.3g, equivalent as salt 1.8g

FISH

garlic and herb salmon

serves 4 / prep time 10 minutes / cook time 20–25 minutes

50g white bread
a few fresh chives, chopped
zest of 1 lemon
4 salmon fillets
100g Philadelphia Garlic & Herbs

PREHEAT the oven to 180°C, gas 4. Place the bread in a food processor and blend into fine breadcrumbs. Stir in the chives and lemon zest.

SPREAD the salmon fillets with a thick layer of Philly and place on a lightly oiled baking tray.

TOP with the flavoured breadcrumbs, lightly pressing them into the Philly. Roast in the oven for 15–20 minutes or until cooked. Serve the salmon with new potatoes and salad leaves or a bunch of watercress.

tip If the fish is a little wet, pat it dry with kitchen towel or dust with flour so that it is easier to spread the Philly on top without it sliding off.

Per serving: energy 358kcal, protein 25.4g, carbohydrate 30.6g, fat 15.7g, equivalent as salt 0.3g

chive and red pepper fish cakes

serves 4 / prep time 20 minutes / cook time 15 minutes

15g butter
1 onion, finely chopped
½ red pepper, finely chopped
400g white fish, minced or finely
    chopped
50g Philadelphia Chives,
    softened
100g fresh breadcrumbs
2 tbsp chopped fresh chives
½ tsp paprika
1 tsp garlic powder (optional)
plain flour, for coating
sunflower oil, for shallow frying

MELT the butter and sauté the onion and pepper for 3–5 minutes. Allow to cool then stir in the minced fish, Philly, breadcrumbs, chives, paprika and garlic. Mix together well.

FORM the mixture into 4 patties, toss in a little flour to coat, and refrigerate until firm.

HEAT a little oil in a frying pan and cook the fish cakes for about 8–10 minutes, turning once until golden and cooked through. Place onto kitchen towel to soak up any excess oil. Serve immediately.

tip For a delicious meal idea serve the fish cakes with potato or vegetable wedges, salad, a spoonful of creamy caper sauce (recipe on page 68) and a slice of lemon.

Per serving: energy 301kcal, protein 28.7g, carbohydrate 25.5g, fat 10.1g, equivalent as salt 1.7g

salmon en croûte

serves 2 / prep time 15 minutes / cook time 25–30 minutes

60g Philadelphia Garlic & Herbs
1 tbsp semi-skimmed milk
2 tsp lemon juice
150g puff pastry, thawed if frozen
2 salmon fillets, skinned
1 egg, beaten
freshly ground black pepper

PREHEAT the oven to 200°C, gas 6. Blend the Philly, milk, lemon juice and black pepper together.

ROLL out the pastry and cut into four oblongs to fit the size of the salmon fillets. Place the fillets on two of the pastry pieces and spoon the Philly mixture onto the salmon. Brush the edges of the pastry with beaten egg, top with the remaining pastry squares and seal the edges together.

BRUSH the top of the salmon parcels with the remaining egg and bake for 25–30 minutes until golden brown. Serve immediately with a green salad or steamed vegetables.

tip You can also make this using Philadelphia Light and mix in your favourite chopped fresh leafy herbs, e.g. basil, parsley or coriander.

Per serving: energy 704kcal, protein 44.0g, carbohydrate 34.4g, fat 45.5g, equivalent as salt 1.4g

piri piri haddock

serves 2 / prep time 10 minutes / cook time 20–25 minutes

2 × 150g pieces haddock loin
50g Philadelphia Light
½ red pepper, finely diced
¼ red chilli, finely chopped
　　and deseeded
2 tbsp red wine vinegar

PREHEAT the oven to 190°C, gas 5. Place the haddock in an ovenproof dish. Mix the Philly, red pepper and chilli together and spread over the top of the fish.

SPOON the vinegar around the fish and cover the dish with foil.

COOK the fish for 10 minutes, remove the foil and cook for a further 10 minutes until the fish is cooked through.

tip If you like tangy flavours add a splash of fresh lime juice to the vinegar. Perfect served with steamed broccoli and green beans.

Per serving: energy 177kcal, protein 31.0g, carbohydrate 3.7g, fat 3.9g, equivalent as salt 0.5g

grilled prawns with mango salsa

serves 4 / prep time 20–25 minutes / cook time 8–10 minutes

100g Philadelphia Light
zest and juice of 1 lime
1 red chilli, finely chopped and
    deseeded
24 tail-on cooked king prawns

For the salsa:
1 ripe mango, peeled and diced
½ red onion, finely chopped
1 tbsp chopped fresh coriander
juice of 1 lime
1 small bag of salad leaves

PREHEAT the grill to medium. In a bowl, mix the Philly, zest and juice of the lime and half the chilli, add the prawns and mix well to coat. Leave to marinate for 20 minutes.

MIX together the salsa ingredients and the remaining chilli and leave on one side.

THREAD the prawns onto 8 skewers and grill for approximately 4–5 minutes turning occasionally until lightly browned. Serve with the salsa and some salad leaves.

tip To make this recipe with uncooked prawns thread them onto the skewers and cook for about 8 minutes until they turn pink all over.

Per serving: energy 121kcal, protein 14.1g, carbohydrate 8.4g, fat 3.6g, equivalent as salt 2.2g

trout with avocado stuffing

serves 2 / prep time 10–12 minutes / cook time 20–25 minutes

2 whole trout, cleaned
juice of ½ lemon

For the stuffing:
½ ripe avocado, flesh diced
4 cherry tomatoes, quartered
60g Philadelphia Garlic & Herbs

PREHEAT the oven to 190°C, gas 5. Mix together the stuffing ingredients.

FILL the trout cavity with the Philly mixture and place into an oiled ovenproof dish. Pour over the lemon juice.

BAKE in a preheated oven for 20–25 minutes until the fish is cooked and flakes easily. Serve with seasonal vegetables.

tip Whole trout are available from major supermarkets or your local fishmonger and they will clean it for you if required.

Per serving: energy 338kcal, protein 36.4g, carbohydrate 2.7g, fat 20.3g, equivalent as salt 0.5g

smoked haddock and sweet potato pie

serves 4 / prep time 15 minutes / cook time 35–40 minutes

1 kg sweet potatoes, peeled
   and cut into 3cm dice
120g Philadelphia Chives
300g smoked haddock
300g haddock loin
2 tbsp semi-skimmed milk

PREHEAT the oven to 190°C, gas 5. Cover the potatoes with water, bring to the boil and cook for approximately 10 minutes or until soft. Drain well and mash with 20g of the Philly, set aside.

PLACE the fish in a microwaveable dish with a teaspoon of milk, cover and microwave on high for approximately 5 minutes or steam for 8–10 minutes until just cooked. Remove skin and any bones, flake the fish and place into a large ovenproof dish.

MIX the remaining Philly with the milk and spoon over the fish. Top with the mashed sweet potato and cook for 20 minutes until the Philly sauce is bubbling around the edge of the dish and the potato is browned.

tip The sweet potato adds a great splash of colour but you can make this with regular mashed potato too.

Per serving: energy 390kcal, protein 34.3g, carbohydrate 54.9g, fat 5.4g, equivalent as salt 2.2g

thai style sea bass

serves 4 / prep time 20 minutes / cook time 15–20 minutes

4 sea bass fillets, each
   cut lengthways into 3
1½ tbsp sunflower oil

For the marinade:
½ tsp fennel seeds
½ tsp coriander seeds
½ tsp chilli flakes
1 clove garlic, crushed
1 tbsp fish sauce
½ tbsp olive oil
pinch sugar

For the dressing:
100g Philadelphia Light
zest and juice of 1 lime
1 tbsp chopped fresh coriander
¼ tsp chilli flakes
½ tbsp olive oil

PLACE all of the dry marinade ingredients into a pestle and mortar and grind well to release the flavours. Stir in the fish sauce and olive oil. Pour over the sea bass fillets and leave for 15 minutes to marinate.

MIX the dressing ingredients and warm in a small pan, do not boil. Put to one side whilst the fish is cooked.

HEAT the oil in a frying pan and fry the sea bass fillets skin side down first, for 2 minutes, turn and cook for a further 1 minute. Serve the fish with the dressing spooned over it on noodles and stir-fried vegetables.

tip If you don't have a pestle and mortar place the ingredients in a sturdy bowl and use the end of a rolling pin to crush them.

Per serving: energy 246kcal, protein 31.4g, carbohydrate 2.7g, fat 12.3g, equivalent as salt 0.9g

CHICKEN

thai green chicken curry

serves 4 / prep time 10 minutes / cook time 20 minutes

2 tsp Thai green curry paste
4 chicken breasts, cut into pieces
1 small onion, finely sliced
1 green pepper, sliced
1 red pepper, finely sliced
120g Philadelphia Extra Light
3–4 tbsp skimmed milk
steamed Thai rice, to serve

HEAT a large non-stick pan and add the Thai curry paste, chicken and onion. Fry for 6–8 minutes until the chicken is cooked through.

ADD the pepper and continue cooking for 3–4 minutes until the pepper softens and the chicken is golden brown.

STIR the Philly and milk through the mixture until melted. Serve with steamed Thai rice.

tip The heat of curry pastes can vary so check before you use it. You can always add a little more if you like a hotter curry.

Per serving: energy 265kcal, protein 46.8g, carbohydrate 7.2g, fat 5.6g, equivalent as salt 0.7g

coriander and lime chicken

serves 4 / prep time 5–10 minutes / cook time 10–15 minutes

4 skinless chicken breasts
100g Philadelphia Light
zest and juice of 2 limes
2 cloves garlic, crushed
3 tbsp chopped fresh coriander
freshly ground black pepper
fresh coriander and lime wedges,
   to garnish

PREHEAT the grill to medium hot. Make 3 or 4 deep cuts in the surface of the chicken breasts.

MIX the Philly, zest and juice of the limes, garlic and coriander in a large bowl, and season with black pepper. Add the chicken to the bowl and coat well with the Philly mixture.

GRILL for approximately 12–15 minutes, turning once or until the juices of the chicken run clear when tested with a skewer. Garnish with a little coriander and lime wedges.

tip This is a lovely light summery recipe – it can be cooked on a hot barbecue for 12–15 minutes and served with salad and chargrilled peppers.

Per serving: energy 190kcal, protein 33.9g, carbohydrate 1.4g, fat 5.5g, equivalent as salt 0.5g

apricot and almond chicken

serves 4 / prep time 15 minutes / cook time 15–20 minutes

1 tsp olive oil
4 chicken breasts, sliced
1 small onion, finely chopped
½ tsp turmeric
½ tsp cinnamon
100g Philadelphia Extra Light
275ml skimmed milk
150g ready-to-eat apricots, halved
50g sultanas
25g flaked almonds

HEAT the oil in a large pan and brown the chicken over a medium heat for approx 5 minutes.

ADD the onion, turmeric and cinnamon. Continue cooking for 3–4 minutes until the chicken is cooked through.

STIR the Philly, milk, apricots, sultanas and almonds into the pan. Cook over a low heat for 8–10 minutes, stirring occasionally until the Philly has melted and the sauce has thickened.

tip Plain or fruity couscous is the perfect accompaniment. To make this fruity couscous stir sprigs of lemon thyme, dried cranberries, sultanas, orange zest and pistachio pieces into the prepared couscous.

Per serving: energy 388kcal, protein 50.4g, carbohydrate 28.5g, fat 8.8g, equivalent as salt 0.53g

herby philly chicken and parma ham

serves 4 / prep time 10 minutes / cook time 20–25 minutes

100g Philadelphia Garlic & Herbs
4 chicken breasts
4 slices of Parma ham
1 bag mixed salad leaves

PREHEAT the oven to 200°C, gas 6. Spread the Philly onto the chicken breasts and lay the Parma ham on top.

PLACE the chicken in a non-stick ovenproof dish and bake for 20–25 minutes until the chicken is thoroughly cooked and the juices run clear when tested with a skewer.

LEAVE to cool slightly and then carefully slice into pieces. Simply serve with the mixed salad.

tip Roasted vine-ripened tomatoes are a great addition to this dish. Simply pop the tomatoes (still on the vine) into the oven 10–15 minutes before the chicken has finished cooking.

Per serving: energy 282kcal, protein 48.4g, carbohydrate 1.6g, fat 9.1g, equivalent as salt 1.3g

chicken with salsa verde

serves 4 / prep time 15 minutes / cook time 40 minutes

4 large chicken breasts
120g Philadelphia, softened
4 anchovies, roughly chopped
2 tbsp finely chopped parsley
2 tbsp roughly chopped capers
8 baby spinach leaves
½ tbsp olive oil

For the salsa verde:
50ml olive oil
2 tbsp finely chopped parsley
2 tbsp finely chopped basil
1 tbsp white wine vinegar
1 tbsp finely chopped green olives
1 tbsp capers, finely chopped
1 tbsp finely chopped gherkins
3 anchovies, finely chopped
1 clove garlic, crushed

PREHEAT the oven to 180°C, gas 4. Cut a long deep slit in one side of each chicken breast to make a pocket. Mix together the Philly, anchovies, parsley and capers. Stuff each chicken breast with one quarter of the Philly mixture and top with spinach leaves. Close and seal with wooden cocktail sticks.

RUB a little oil over the chicken breasts. Transfer the chicken to a baking tray and bake for about 25 minutes or until the chicken is cooked and the juices run clear when tested with a skewer.

COMBINE all the salsa verde ingredients in a bowl and spoon over the chicken to serve.

tip For a quicker version, spoon a little pesto over the chicken instead of making the salsa verde.

Per serving: energy 432kcal, protein 48.3g, carbohydrate 1.5g, fat 25.9g, equivalent as salt 1.4g

stir-fried chicken tortillas

serves 4 / prep time 15 minutes / cook time 15 minutes

1 tsp olive or sunflower oil
4 chicken breasts, sliced
1 onion, thinly sliced
1 red pepper, thinly sliced
4 soft flour tortillas
120g Philadelphia Extra Light
2 tbsp skimmed milk
½ tsp paprika
pinch cayenne
1 small bag mixed lettuce leaves
12 cherry tomatoes, halved

PREHEAT the oven to 190°C, gas 5. Heat the oil in a large non-stick frying pan. Add the chicken and brown over a medium heat for approximately 5 minutes. Add the onion and pepper, cook for a further 5 minutes or until cooked through.

WARM the tortillas as directed on the pack, then drape each tortilla over up-turned ramekins or ovenproof teacups on a baking tray. Heat the tortillas in the preheated oven for 5–8 minutes until they have become crisp. Leave to cool, then remove from the ramekins or cups.

WHISK together the Philly, milk, paprika and cayenne and add to the chicken mixture. Continue cooking for 2 minutes to heat through. Place the lettuce and tomatoes in the bottom of each tortilla cup and top with the chicken mixture. Serve immediately.

tip Turkey is a lower fat alternative to chicken and strips of turkey breast can be used in this recipe.

Per serving: energy 459kcal, protein 61.8g, carbohydrate 42.1g, fat 5.9g, equivalent as salt 1.1g

RICE

creamy mushroom risotto

serves 4 / prep time 10–12 minutes / cook time 30 minutes

2 tsp olive oil
200g risotto rice
600ml hot good quality
    vegetable stock
350g mixed mushrooms, cut into
    large pieces
1 clove garlic, crushed
120g Philadelphia Light
a little skimmed milk (optional)
a handful of fresh parsley, roughly
    chopped
freshly ground black pepper

HEAT 1 teaspoon of the oil in a saucepan. Add the rice and gently fry over a medium heat for 2 minutes or until lightly golden. Gradually add the stock and 300ml hot water, then bring to the boil. Simmer for 20 minutes or until tender and all the liquid is absorbed. Add a little more water if required during cooking.

HEAT the remaining olive oil in a frying pan and add the mushrooms and garlic. Fry for 4–5 minutes, until starting to brown.

STIR the Philly into the cooked rice. If the mixture is too thick add a little milk. Remove the rice from the heat and stir in the mushrooms, parsley and black pepper to taste. Serve immediately.

tip Choose your favourite type of mushrooms for this dish – a mixture of chestnut, shiitake and oyster mushrooms works well.

Per serving: energy 377kcal, protein 12.2g, carbohydrate 62.1g, fat 8.9g, equivalent as salt 1.8g

asparagus and smoked ham risotto

serves 4 / prep time 5–10 minutes / cook time 30–35 minutes

1 tbsp olive oil
1 red onion, chopped
150g cooked smoked ham,
    cubed
300g risotto rice
100g asparagus, cut into
    2–3cm pieces
750ml hot good quality
    vegetable stock
100g Philadelphia Light

HEAT the oil in a large pan, fry the onion and ham for 2–3 minutes until the onion has softened and begun to brown.

ADD the rice and asparagus to the pan and cook for 1 minute, stirring all the time.

ADD the hot stock, over a moderate heat, stirring well after each addition, allowing the liquid to be absorbed by the rice before adding more.

CONTINUE until all the liquid is used up and the rice is cooked through (if the rice is not quite cooked it may be necessary to add more liquid, or if there is too much liquid, allow it to bubble off). Remove from the heat, add the Philly and stir well to produce a creamy risotto. Serve immediately.

tip This dish is also lovely with parma ham or crispy bacon instead of the cooked ham.

Per serving: energy 392kcal, protein 15.7g, carbohydrate 64.0g, fat 8.1g, equivalent as salt 2.7g

green bean and mint risotto

serves 4 / prep time 5 minutes / cook time 30–35 minutes

1 tbsp olive oil
1 onion, chopped
300g risotto rice
100g fresh or frozen baby
    broad beans
100g fresh or frozen peas
750ml hot good quality
    vegetable stock
120g Philadelphia Garlic & Herbs
1 tbsp finely chopped fresh mint
freshly ground black pepper
Parmesan shavings, to serve

HEAT the oil in a large pan, add the onion and fry for 1–2 minutes, until beginning to soften, add the rice and cook for 1 minute. Add the beans and peas, stir well.

ADD the hot stock gradually, over a moderate heat, stirring well after each addition, allowing the liquid to be absorbed by the rice before adding more.

CONTINUE until all of the liquid is used up and the rice has cooked through (it may be necessary to add a little more liquid if it isn't quite cooked or if there is too much liquid, allow it to bubble off).

STIR in the Philly and mint and remove from the heat. Season with freshly ground black pepper and serve with Parmesan shavings.

tip This dish can be served as a main course or as an accompaniment to grilled white fish or chicken.

Per serving: energy 401kcal, protein 12.0g, carbohydrate 67.1g, fat 9.7g, equivalent as salt 1.7g

pork and mushroom stroganoff

serves 4 / prep time 10 minutes / cook time 20–25 minutes

225g brown rice
2 tbsp olive or sunflower oil
450g pork tenderloin fillet,
    sliced into strips
1 red onion, chopped
225g chestnut mushrooms, sliced
1 tbsp fresh sage, chopped
2 tbsp white wine
1 tsp wholegrain mustard
120g Philadelphia Light
freshly ground black pepper

COOK the rice according to the instructions on the pack and while it is cooking prepare the stroganoff.

HEAT the oil in a large, deep frying pan and fry the pork in two batches over a high heat, browning on all sides. Remove the pork from the pan and set aside.

FRY the onion, mushrooms and sage for 2–3 minutes until beginning to brown.

STIR in the wine, mustard and Philly and stir well until all of the Philly has been incorporated. Return the pork to the pan, heat through, season with pepper and serve with the rice.

tip As an alternative use a mixture of wild and long grain rice instead of the brown rice.

Per serving: energy 536kcal, protein 43.4g, carbohydrate 50.8g, fat 18.4g, equivalent as salt 0.6g

chicken biryani

serves 4 / prep time 5–10 minutes / cook time 20–25 minutes

1 tbsp olive or sunflower oil
1 large onion, chopped
2 chicken breasts, diced
1 medium courgette, diced
1 tbsp curry powder or paste
225g easy cook rice
550ml hot good quality
    chicken stock
120g Philadelphia Light
25g flaked almonds, toasted

HEAT the oil in a deep pan, fry the onion until beginning to brown. Add the chicken to the pan and brown on all sides.

ADD the courgette and curry powder and fry for 1 minute, then add the rice and stir well.

POUR in the hot stock and add the Philly. Stir, put the lid on and reduce the heat to low. Cook for 15 minutes or until the rice is cooked through, stirring once or twice during the cooking time. Add a little more liquid if it becomes too dry. Serve with the almonds sprinkled on top.

tip Adjust the heat level by choosing a curry powder or paste to suit your taste.

Per serving: energy 467kcal, protein 29.0g, carbohydrate 55.7g, fat 15.7g, equivalent as salt 1.4g

VEGETABLES

stuffed roasted red peppers

serves 4 / prep time 5–10 minutes / cook time 30–35 minutes

4 large red peppers
12 sun-dried tomatoes, roughly
    chopped
2 garlic cloves, roughly chopped
2 tbsp olive oil
200g risotto rice
100g Philadelphia, softened
3 tsp red pesto
25g pine nuts, toasted
rocket or salad leaves, to serve

PREHEAT the oven to 200°C, gas 6. Halve the red peppers and remove the seeds. Combine the sun-dried tomatoes and garlic, divide among the pepper halves and drizzle over the olive oil. Place onto a baking tray and roast in the oven for 20–25 minutes.

COOK the risotto rice as directed on the pack. When cooked, stir in the Philly, pesto and pine nuts.

REMOVE the peppers from the oven and leave to cool slightly. Scoop out the tomato and garlic mixture and stir into the rice.

SPOON the rice mixture into the pepper halves and return to the oven for 5 minutes or until heated through. Serve with fresh rocket leaves or side salad.

tip These peppers are also delicious served chilled with crusty bread for a summer lunch.

Per serving: energy 564kcal, protein 9.9g, carbohydrate 52.5g, fat 35.3g, equivalent as salt 1.2g

butternut, cauliflower and chickpea curry

serves 4 / prep time 15 minutes / cook time 25 minutes

1 tbsp olive oil
1 large onion, peeled and cut
    into thin wedges
1 tbsp korma curry paste
1kg butternut squash, peeled
    and cut into 2–3cm cubes
¼ medium cauliflower, cut into
    florets
2 large Desiree potatoes, cut into
    2–3cm cubes
410g can chopped tomatoes
225g can chickpeas, drained
375ml good quality vegetable stock
2 tbsp desiccated coconut
125g Philadelphia Light, softened
25g fresh coriander, roughly
    chopped
1–2 tsp lemon juice
steamed rice, to serve

HEAT the oil in a large saucepan. Add the onion and cook gently for 5 minutes or until the onion is soft and lightly browned. Add the curry paste, stir well and cook for another minute, or until fragrant.

ADD the vegetables, chickpeas, stock and coconut. Bring the mixture to the boil, simmer, covered over a low heat for about 15 minutes or until the vegetables are just tender.

STIR through the Philly until blended. Add the coriander and lemon juice to taste. Serve immediately with steamed rice.

tip Substitute the butternut squash for pumpkin when it is in season.

Per serving: energy 626kcal, protein 19.6g, carbohydrate 83.1g, fat 26.1g, equivalent as salt 2.3g

broccoli gratin

serves 4 / prep time 5 minutes / cook time 10–12 minutes

300g broccoli, cut into florets
60g Philadelphia Light
1 tbsp pesto
25g wholemeal breadcrumbs
25g Cheddar cheese, grated

COOK the broccoli in boiling water for 4–5 minutes or until tender. Drain well and put into an ovenproof dish.

MIX the Philly with the pesto and spoon over the broccoli.

PREHEAT the grill to medium. Top the Philly mixture with the breadcrumbs and cheese and grill for 5 minutes or until browned.

tip Leeks, cauliflower or fennel work really well as an alternative to broccoli.

Per serving: energy 121kcal, protein 8.1g, carbohydrate 4.8g, fat 7.9g, equivalent as salt 0.5g

leek and garlic gratin

serves 8 / prep time 20–25 minutes / cook time 45 minutes

2 tsp olive oil
1 small onion, thinly chopped
450g leeks, washed and sliced
2 garlic cloves, crushed
180g Philadelphia Light, softened
200ml semi-skimmed milk
2 tsp wholegrain mustard
450g waxy potatoes, peeled
    and just cooked
75g Cheddar, grated
freshly ground black pepper

PREHEAT the oven to 200°C, gas 6. Lightly grease a 1 litre ovenproof dish.

HEAT the oil in a large saucepan and gently fry the onion, leeks and garlic until soft. Add the Philly, milk and mustard to the leek mixture, season with black pepper. Gently heat, stirring occasionally until the Philly has melted.

SLICE the potatoes thinly and arrange half on the base of the ovenproof dish. Top the potatoes with half the leek mixture and repeat with the remaining potato slices and leek mixture.

SPRINKLE with the grated Cheddar and bake for about 20 minutes or until the top is golden.

tip Waxy potatoes (e.g. Maris Peer or Charlotte) are best for this recipe as they are firm and hold their shape well.

Per serving: energy 165kcal, protein 7.9g, carbohydrate 15.1g, fat 8.5g, equivalent as salt 0.6g

garlic and herb mash

serves 4 / prep time 10 minutes / cook time 30 minutes

450g floury potatoes, peeled
100g Philadelphia Garlic & Herbs,
    softened
a dash of semi-skimmed milk
    (optional)
fresh herbs, to garnish

CUT the potatoes into 3cm chunks and place in a large pan of water. Bring to the boil and cook for 15–20 minutes or until tender.

DRAIN and mash the potatoes together with the Philly and add a little milk if you like a softer consistency. Serve warm, garnished with a few fresh herbs.

tip Floury potatoes (e.g. Desiree or King Edward) are best used for mashing as they are softer and have a dry texture, which makes lovely fluffy mash.

Per serving: energy 120kcal, protein 4.1g, carbohydrate 20.1g, fat 3.0g, equivalent as salt 0.3g

carrot and sweet potato mash

serves 6 / prep time 10 minutes / cook time 30 minutes

450g carrots, peeled
2 medium sweet potatoes,
    peeled
100g Philadelphia Chives,
    softened
a few fresh chives, to garnish
    (optional)

CUT the vegetables into 2–3cm chunks. Place the carrots in a large pan of boiling water and cook for 5 minutes.

ADD the sweet potato and continue cooking for 20–25 minutes or until tender. Drain the vegetables.

MASH the vegetables together until smooth, then swirl through the Philly. Serve warm, garnished with a few fresh chives if desired.

tip Substitute any root vegetable (e.g. parsnips, swede or turnip) for the carrot and sweet potato to make a mash of your choice.

Per serving: energy 63kcal, protein 2.1g, carbohydrate 8.8g, fat 2.4g, equivalent as salt 0.3g

roasted vegetable couscous

serves 4 / prep time 20 minutes / cook time 30 minutes

1 small aubergine
1 yellow pepper, cored
    and deseeded
1 red onion, peeled
1 tbsp olive oil
200g couscous
2 tbsp skimmed milk
75g Philadelphia Extra Light,
    softened
a little fresh mint
zest and juice of 1 lemon

PREHEAT the oven to 220°C, gas 7. Cut the vegetables into 2–3cm chunks, toss in the oil and place in a roasting tin. Cook for 25–30 minutes or until starting to go golden around the edges.

MAKE up the couscous as directed on the packet.

STIR the milk into the Philly a little at a time. Add the fresh mint, lemon juice and zest. Leave to stand whilst you stir the vegetables into the couscous and then drizzle with the Philly dressing to serve.

tip This can be made in advance and served cold. Pour the dressing over just before serving.

Per serving: energy 280kcal, protein 10.8g, carbohydrate 46.7g, fat 6.0g, equivalent as salt 2.0g

Philly's mild and creamy taste works surprisingly well in sweet dishes too. It blends quickly and easily, ideal for combining with fresh and fruity ingredients or luxurious chocolate for more indulgent desserts. Perfect treats to share with friends and family.

SWEET TREATS

classic philly frosting

makes enough to ice a 21cm cake / prep time 5 minutes

200g Philadelphia
25g icing sugar, sieved
1 tsp vanilla extract

BEAT the Philly in a small bowl until softened and stir in the sieved icing sugar.

ADD the vanilla extract and stir until combined.

tip For a really special occasion scrape out a vanilla pod with the back of a sharp knife and add the seeds to the icing instead of the vanilla extract.

Per recipe: energy 598kcal, protein 11.8g, carbohydrate 32.6g, fat 48.0g, equivalent as salt 2.0g

creamy coffee frosting

makes enough to ice and fill a 21cm cake / prep time 5 minutes

2 tsp instant coffee
4 tbsp caster sugar
200g Philadelphia Light
150ml double cream

DISSOLVE the instant coffee and caster sugar in 1 tbsp water, then beat into the Philly.

WHISK the double cream to form soft peaks, then fold into the Philly mixture.

tip This is perfect to use as a filling and frosting for a home-made coffee cake.

Per recipe: energy 1372kcal, protein 19.4g, carbohydrate 94.9g, fat 103.6g, equivalent as salt 2.1g

sticky toffee filling

makes enough to fill an 18cm cake / prep time 5 minutes

200g Philadelphia Light
50g dulce de leche (toffee
    fudge sauce)

BEAT the Philly until softened. Stir in the dulce de leche until thoroughly mixed. Cover and chill until required.

tip For a quick banoffee dessert place crushed digestive biscuits in serving dish, add some of the sticky toffee filling and top with banana slices.

Per recipe: energy 450kcal, protein 18.6g, carbohydrate 37.9g, fat 25.4g, equivalent as salt 2.0g

lemon and raspberry filling

makes enough to fill an 18cm cake / prep time 5 minutes

200g Philadelphia Light
3 tablespoons lemon curd
150g fresh raspberries

BEAT the Philly until softened and stir in the lemon curd. Gently fold in the raspberries.

tip Use to fill a Victoria sponge or chocolate cake, or simply serve a spoonful of the filling with a slice of sponge cake. As an alternative use fresh blackberries in the autumn for this filling.

Per recipe: energy 771kcal, protein 19.4g, carbohydrate 109.2g, fat 30.8g, equivalent as salt 2.2g

cheesecake brownies

serves 12 / prep time 10 minutes / cook time 35–40 minutes

125g butter
125g dark chocolate, chopped
200g soft brown sugar
3 eggs, lightly beaten
50g plain flour, sifted
50g cocoa powder
¼ tsp baking powder
200g Philadelphia Light
50g caster sugar

PREHEAT the oven to 180°C, gas 4. Grease and line an 18 x 28cm rectangular tin. Combine the butter, chocolate and brown sugar in a medium saucepan. Stir over a medium heat until the chocolate and butter have melted. Remove from the heat and whisk in the eggs.

ADD the flour, cocoa, and baking powder and stir until well combined. Pour into the prepared tin.

BEAT the Philly and caster sugar until smooth and creamy. Spoon randomly over the chocolate mixture and swirl with the tip of a knife. Bake for 35–40 minutes or until cooked through. Allow to cool before slicing.

Per serving: energy 282kcal, protein 4.9g, carbohydrate 32.4g, fat 15.9g, equivalent as salt 0.5g

toblerone chocolate truffles

serves 24 / prep time 30 minutes / chilling time 1 hour

200g Philadelphia
1½ tbsp soured cream
½ tbsp clear honey
½ tbsp amaretto (optional)
100g dark Toblerone
60g chopped toasted almonds
cocoa powder, sieved for rolling

BEAT the Philly, soured cream, honey and amaretto with an electric mixer in a small bowl until light and creamy.

BREAK up the Toblerone and place in a heatproof bowl over a pan of gently simmering water. Stir until melted. Fold the melted chocolate and almonds into the Philly mixture. Refrigerate for at least 1 hour before rolling (otherwise the mixture will be quite sticky).

SHAPE into 24 teaspoon-sized balls and roll in cocoa powder. Chill for at least 20 minutes before serving.

Per serving: energy 66kcal, protein 1.3g, carbohydrate 3.9g, fat 5.1g, equivalent as salt 0.1g

carrot cake

serves 10 / prep time 20–25 minutes / cook time 60 minutes

2 eggs, separated
225g soft brown sugar
175g butter or margarine,
    melted
150g wholemeal flour
1 tsp baking powder
½ tsp mixed spice
25g chopped walnuts
25g sultanas
175g carrots, grated

For the topping:
200g Philadelphia
50g icing sugar, sieved
finely grated zest of ½ lemon

PREHEAT the oven to 190°C, gas 5. Grease and line the base of a 20cm cake tin.

CREAM together the egg yolks, sugar and melted butter. Stir in 2 tablespoons warm water. Place the remaining cake ingredients in a bowl, make a well in the centre, add the egg mixture and beat thoroughly.

WHISK the egg whites until standing in soft peaks. Fold carefully into the cake mixture. Spoon the mixture into the prepared tin and bake for 45–50 minutes or until a skewer inserted in the centre comes out clean. Turn out and cool on a wire rack.

CREAM together the Philly and sieved icing sugar until soft and creamy. Stir in the lemon zest and swirl over the cake. Decorate with a little more grated lemon zest if desired.

tip Leave the cake to cool a little in the tin to make it easier to turn out.

Per serving: energy 374kcal, protein 5.0g, carbohydrate 41.7g, fat 22.4g, equivalent as salt 0.7g

5-minute fruit brûlée

serves 6 / prep time 10 minutes / cook time 5 minutes

200g Philadelphia Light
150g 0% fat Greek yoghurt
175g ripe soft fruit (e.g. raspberries,
    strawberries, blackberries,
    blueberries)
6 tbsp fruit compote
6 tbsp demerara sugar

PREHEAT the grill to high. Beat together the Philly and Greek yoghurt until well combined.

CUT any larger berries into small pieces. Mix all the berries with the fruit compote and divide between 6 large ramekin dishes. Spoon over the Philly mixture and smooth with the back of a spoon.

SPOON the brown sugar evenly over the Philly and place on a baking tray. Pop under the grill until the sugar is bubbling and has caramelised. Leave for a few minutes to allow the sugar to crisp and cool a little before eating.

tip This can also be made with frozen fruit. Thaw the fruit at room temperature and use as above, draining away any excess juice if necessary.

Per serving: energy 174kcal, protein 4.9g, carbohydrate 31.4g, fat 4.0g, equivalent as salt 0.4g

tiramisù

serves 6 / prep time 15 minutes / chilling time 3–4 hours or overnight

115g sponge fingers
100ml espresso, chilled
½ tbsp amaretto
200g Philadelphia
100ml natural yoghurt
1 tsp vanilla essence
25g icing sugar
2–3 tsp cocoa powder,
  sieved

LINE a small loaf tin with clingfilm. Place the espresso, 50ml water and amaretto in a shallow bowl and set aside. Beat together the Philly, yoghurt, vanilla and icing sugar until softened.

DIP half the sponge fingers in the coffee mixture and line the base of the loaf tin with them. Spread half of the Philly mixture over the sponges in the tin and then repeat to make a second layer.

COVER and leave in the fridge for 3–4 hours or preferably overnight. Dust the top with a thick layer of cocoa powder, then carefully lift the Tiramisù out of the tin using the clingflim. Carefully slice before serving.

tip This dessert is best left overnight to chill so that the flavours fully develop.

Per serving: energy 201kcal, protein 5.0g, carbohydrate 23.3g, fat 9.7g, equivalent as salt 1.1g

grilled peaches with marsala cream

serves 4 / prep time 10 minutes / cook time 8 minutes

120g Philadelphia Light, softened
1 tbsp caster sugar
½ tbsp Marsala or sherry
4 large ripe peaches
2 tbsp soft brown sugar
20g flaked almonds, toasted

BEAT the Philly, caster sugar and Marsala until smooth. Cover and refrigerate.

PREHEAT the grill to high. Cut each peach in half and remove the stone. Sprinkle the cut side with the brown sugar. Place the peaches on a baking tray and pop under a hot grill, cook for 6–8 minutes or until the peaches have softened and the sugar is bubbling and golden.

ARRANGE peaches on serving plates, sprinkle with the almonds and serve with a spoonful of Marsala Philly cream. Serve immediately.

tip Alternatively replace the brown sugar with a dusting of icing sugar and pop the peaches onto a hot barbecue until softened and golden.

Per serving: energy 185kcal, protein 5.0g, carbohydrate 28.5g, fat 6.4g, equivalent as salt 0.3g

summer berry charlotte

serves 8 / prep time 20–25 minutes / chilling time 2–3 hours or overnight

25–30 sponge fingers
290g can mixed berries in syrup,
    drained and syrup reserved
5g powdered gelatine (about
    half a sachet)
200g Philadelphia Light,
    softened
1 tbsp caster sugar
125ml double cream
225g strawberries, halved
    or quartered
fresh raspberries, to serve
raspberry sauce, to serve

LINE a small loaf tin with clingfilm. Trim the sponge fingers to line the base and sides of the tin, leaving the remaining fingers for the top. Reserve about one third of the syrup. Dip the sponges in the remaining syrup and line the tin with them straight away.

DISSOLVE the gelatine in 100ml water, over a pan of hot water. Beat the Philly and sugar in a bowl with an electric mixer until smooth. Stir in the cream and gelatine mixture. Fold in the mixed berries and strawberries. Pour the mixture into the prepared tin. Top with the reserved fingers and brush with the reserved syrup.

CHILL for 2–3 hours or overnight until set. Invert onto a serving plate and serve sliced, with fresh raspberries and raspberry sauce, if desired.

tip Work quickly when you are dipping the sponges into the syrup or they may fall apart. Not all of the sponge fingers have to be dipped as they will absorb liquid from the Philly mixture as it sets.

Per serving: energy 268kcal, protein 5.3g, carbohydrate 34.5g, fat 12.2g, equivalent as salt 1.1g

lemon and philly friands

serves 9 / prep time 15–20 minutes / cook time 15–20 minutes

Filling:
100g Philadelphia Extra Light
½ tbsp icing sugar
zest and juice of ½ small lemon

Friand mixture:
150g icing sugar
50g plain flour
100g ground almonds
grated zest of 1 lemon
125g unsalted butter or
    margarine
4 egg whites
sieved icing sugar, to serve

PREHEAT the oven to 190˚C, gas 5. Lightly grease a 9-hole muffin tin. To make the filling, beat together the Philly, icing sugar, lemon zest and juice. Cover and leave in the fridge to chill.

SIFT the icing sugar and flour into a large bowl. Stir in the ground almonds, lemon zest and melted butter. Beat the egg whites with an electric hand whisk until soft peaks are formed. Gently stir a little of the egg whites into the almond mixture to loosen it, then gently fold in the remaining egg whites.

SPOON into the muffin tin and bake for 15–20 minutes or until golden. Leave to rest in the tin for 5 minutes before removing onto a cooling rack. When cooled slice the tops and fill with the Philly mixture. Dust with a little icing sugar to serve.

tip These delicious cakes are best served warm from the oven, but they can be made a day in advance. Store in an airtight container and fill just before serving.

Per serving: energy 278kcal, protein 5.6g, carbohydrate 24.3g, fat 18.3g, equivalent as salt 0.2g

lemon crêpes

serves 10 / prep time 20 minutes / cook time 30 minutes

125g plain flour
3 eggs, lightly beaten
250ml semi-skimmed milk
200g Philadelphia Light, softened
125g cottage cheese
100g sultanas
2 tbsp caster sugar
grated zest of 1 lemon
20g butter
icing sugar, to dust

SIFT the flour into a medium bowl. Make a well in the centre and gradually whisk in the beaten eggs and milk until smooth. Refrigerate for 30 minutes.

COMBINE the Philly, cottage cheese, sultanas, sugar, and lemon zest until smooth.

MELT the butter in a small non-stick frying pan. When it is hot pour a little of the batter evenly into the pan. Cook the pancake until lightly browned underneath, then turn over and cook the other side until golden. Set aside and repeat to make a total of 10 pancakes, layering them between greaseproof paper.

SPOON two tablespoons of the Philly mixture into the centre of each pancake. Fold the sides of the pancake in to make a parcel and dust with a little icing sugar to serve.

tip Serve with a warm filling by arranging the parcels in an ovenproof dish. Heat through in a 150°C, gas 2 preheated oven for 5 minutes before dusting with icing sugar. Alternatively, serve with a delicious lemon sauce: combine 2 tablespoons butter, a little lemon juice and 2 tablespoons sugar in a pan and simmer for 2 minutes. Drizzle over the warm parcels and serve.

Per serving: energy 179kcal, protein 7.4g, carbohydrate 23.3g, fat 6.8g, equivalent as salt 0.4g

philly bircher muesli

serves 4 / prep time 10 minutes / chilling time at least 1 hour, ideally overnight

100g rolled oats
250ml apple and mango juice
    or cloudy apple juice
2 eating apples, grated
100g Philadelphia Light,
    softened
½ tsp ground cinnamon
75g hazelnuts, toasted
    and roughly chopped

To serve:
fresh or frozen blueberries
apple slices
nectarine slices

COMBINE the oats, juice and grated apple. Leave to soak for at least 1 hour or for best results overnight.

STIR through the Philly, cinnamon and hazelnuts. Spoon into serving bowls.

GARNISH with blueberries, nectarines and extra apple slices to serve.

tip Any fresh fruit can be added just before serving – choose seasonal fresh fruit or your favourite stewed fruit.

Per serving: energy 313kcal, protein 8.0g, carbohydrate 33.3g, fat 17.2g, equivalent as salt 0.3g

frosty apricot ice cream

serves 8–10 / prep time 15 minutes / chilling time 3–4 hours or overnight

425g can apricots, in juice
150g Philadelphia, softened
500g fresh chilled custard

DRAIN the apricots, reserving the juice. Finely chop the apricots.

PLACE the Philly in a bowl with 2–3 tablespoons of the fruit juice. Beat until soft and creamy, then gradually stir in the apricots and custard.

SPOON into a freezerproof container. Place in the freezer until frozen, stirring occasionally, or ideally overnight. Remove from the freezer about 30 minutes before serving to soften.

tip Alternatively, place in an ice-cream maker until frozen or freeze the ice cream mixture in a loaf tin, remove 30 minutes before serving and serve in slices.

Per serving: energy 126kcal, protein 3.1g, carbohydrate 15.3g, fat 6.4g, equivalent as salt 0.3g

Cheesecake wouldn't be cheesecake without Philadelphia. It's an essential ingredient whether you are making a chilled or baked variety. Here you'll find a fabulous choice of our favourite Philly cheesecake recipes, from the classics to the more adventurous, for you to enjoy.

DIVINE
CHEESE
CAKES

10-second cheesecake ideas

Use the ideas below for a sweet treat or turn them into cheesecake sundaes to serve to friends.

10-second cheesecake

SPREAD a layer of Philly onto a digestive biscuit and top with your favourite fresh fruit e.g. sliced strawberries.

gingernut cheesecake

TOP gingernut biscuits with Philly, a couple of banana slices and a little grated chocolate for an indulgent pud.

cookie cheesecake

SPREAD the Philly over chocolate chip cookies and top with fresh raspberries or your favourite fruit pieces.

oaty cheesecake

SPREAD Philly over sweet oaty cookies and then top with pieces of fresh or dried apricots. You can also add juicy sultanas.

tip For mini cheesecake sundaes, crush the biscuits and place in the bottom of a small glass. Beat the Philly until softened, add a little sieved icing sugar and top with the fruits to serve.

BAKED

baked lemon and sultana cheesecake

serves 10 / prep time 25–30 minutes plus overnight chilling / cook time 1–2 hours

50g self-raising flour
½ tsp baking powder
50g soft margarine or butter
275g caster sugar
5 large eggs
400g Philadelphia, softened
40g plain flour
grated zest and juice of 1 lemon
75g sultanas
142ml carton soured cream

PREHEAT oven to 170°C, gas 3. Grease and line the base of a 22cm springform cake tin. Sift the self raising flour and baking powder into a bowl. Add the fat, 50g of the sugar and 1 egg. Mix well then beat for 2–3 minutes. Spread the mixture over the base of the prepared tin.

SEPARATE the remaining eggs. Whisk together the egg yolks and remaining sugar until thick and creamy. Add to the Philly and mix in well. Fold the plain flour into the Philly mixture along with the lemon zest and juice, sultanas and soured cream.

WHISK the egg whites until stiff then fold into the cheese mixture. Pour this over the base mix in the tin. Bake for 1–1¼ hours until firm yet spongy to the touch. Turn the oven off and leave the cheesecake in the oven for 1 hour with the door ajar. Remove the cheesecake from the oven and leave to cool. Chill in the fridge, preferably overnight, before serving.

tip This cheesecake is best left to chill in the fridge overnight or it can be a little soft and sticky to slice.

Per serving: energy 376kcal, protein 8.0g, carbohydrate 42.9g, fat 20.4g, equivalent as salt 0.7g

baked pear and vanilla cheesecake

serves 12 / prep time 25 minutes plus chilling time / cook time 1¼ hours

150g gingernut biscuits, crushed
50g butter or soft margarine,
    melted
600g Philadelphia, softened
225g caster sugar
3 eggs, lightly beaten
1 vanilla pod
200ml single cream
410g can pear halves,
    well drained and sliced

PREHEAT the oven to 150°C, gas 2. Grease and line the base of a 20cm springform cake tin. Combine the biscuit crumbs and butter and press into the base of the prepared tin. Chill.

BEAT the Philly and sugar until smooth, add the eggs and mix until combined. Split the vanilla pod lengthwise and scrape the seeds out into the cream, gently fold through the mixture. Pour onto the prepared base. Bake for $1\,^1/_4$ hours.

ALLOW the cheesecake to cool completely in the oven. Place the pear slices onto the cheesecake and chill before serving.

tip This can also be made in individual mini cheesecake tins or ovenproof dishes.

Per serving: energy 342kcal, protein 5.9g, carbohydrate 33.3g, fat 21.6g, equivalent as salt 0.7g

peach cheesecake muffins

serves 12 / prep time 10–12 minutes / cook time 25–30 minutes

400g Philadelphia, softened
200g caster sugar
2 eggs
150g ground almonds
125ml soured cream
2 tbsp custard powder
2 medium peaches, sliced,
    or ½ × 440g can peach
    slices, drained
2 tbsp maple syrup

LINE the bases of a 12 cup large muffin tin and grease well. Preheat the oven to 180°C, gas 4.

BEAT the Philly and sugar in a medium bowl until combined. Add the eggs, ground almonds, soured cream and custard powder and beat until smooth. Spoon into the prepared tin. Top each muffin with peach slices, and drizzle with maple syrup.

BAKE for 25–30 minutes or until set and golden. Leave to cool before removing from the tin.

tip These are also divine eaten warm, served straight from the tin.

Per serving: energy 290kcal, protein 6.3g, carbohydrate 27.0g, fat 18.2g, equivalent as salt 0.4g

baked chocolate and orange cheesecake

serves 12 / prep time 20–25 minutes plus chilling time / cook time 1 hour

150g butter
150g orange-flavoured
    chocolate biscuits, crushed
75g caster sugar
2 eggs, separated
450g Philadelphia Light, softened
1½ tbsp warm water
15g cocoa powder, sifted
1 tbsp custard powder
4 tbsp single cream
finely grated zest and juice
    of ½ orange
icing sugar, orange rind and
    chocolate curls, to decorate

PREHEAT the oven to 160°C, gas 3. Grease and line the base of a 22cm springform cake tin. Melt 50g of the butter. Stir the melted butter into the biscuit crumbs and press into the tin. Chill until required.

CREAM together the remaining butter and the sugar until light and fluffy. Gradually beat in the egg yolks and then the softened Philly. In a separate bowl mix the warm water, cocoa and custard powder together to form a firm paste. Slowly add the single cream to the paste and then combine with the Philly mixture. Gradually add the orange zest and juice, stir until evenly mixed.

WHISK the egg whites until stiff and fold gently into the mixture. Pour onto the biscuit base and bake for 1 hour. Leave the cheesecake to cool completely in the oven. Decorate the top with a sprinkling of sieved icing sugar, orange rind and chocolate curls.

tip Leaving the cheesecake in the oven to cool completely reduces the risk of it cracking.

Per serving: energy 275kcal, protein 5.5g, carbohydrate 19.7g, fat 19.8g, equivalent as salt 0.8g

CHILLED

apricot crumble cheesecake

serves 12 / prep time 20–25 minutes / setting time 2 hours

For the base:
150g sweet oaty biscuits, crushed
60g butter or margarine, melted
50g roasted hazelnuts, finely
    chopped
1 tsp cinnamon
½ tsp nutmeg

For the topping:
400g Philadelphia, softened
150g caster sugar
1 × 11g sachet of gelatine
2 tbsp lemon juice
250ml double cream, lightly
    whipped
410g can apricot halves in fruit
    juice, drained and halved

COMBINE the biscuit crumbs, butter, hazelnuts and spices. Divide this in half (saving the other half) and press into the base of a 20cm springform cake tin. Chill until firm.

BEAT together the Philly and sugar until smooth.

DISSOLVE the gelatine in 3 tablespoons (or 75ml) of water, over a pan of hot water. Beat the gelatine and lemon juice into the cheese mixture until well blended. Fold in the whipped cream and apricots. Pour the mixture over the biscuit crumb in the tin.

TOP the cheesecake with the remaining crumb mixture. Chill for 2 hours or until set. Serve straight from the fridge.

tip For a variation on the classic biscuit base, mix a tablespoon of desiccated coconut into the biscuit crumbs.

Per serving: energy 369kcal, protein 4.8g, carbohydrate 24.7g, fat 28.7g, equivalent as salt 0.5g

vanilla and vodka cheesecake

serves 10 / prep time 25 minutes / setting time 2–3 hours

1 vanilla pod or 2 tsp vanilla
    extract
175g caster sugar
75ml vodka
400g Philadelphia, softened
3 rounded tsp powdered gelatine
284ml double cream, lightly
    whipped

LINE the base of a 20cm springform tin. Split the vanilla pod lengthwise and scrape out the seeds with a knife. Combine the vanilla seeds and pod or vanilla extract, 60g of the sugar and vodka in a small saucepan. Stir over a low heat until the sugar is dissolved. Bring the mixture to the boil, and simmer for 1 minute. Cool, then discard the vanilla pod.

BEAT the Philly and remaining sugar in a large bowl with an electric mixer until smooth. Add the vodka syrup.

DISSOLVE the gelatine in 4 tablespoons of water, over a pan of hot water and mix well. Stir into the vodka mixture. Gently fold in the whipped cream until combined. Pour the mixture into the prepared tin. Refrigerate for 2–3 hours or until set.

tip This cheesecake doesn't have a biscuit base so it is perfect accompanied by small, crisp biscuits such as shortbread or thin almond biscuits. Top with soft fruit and a little fruit coulis to serve.

Per serving: energy 290kcal, protein 4.4g, carbohydrate 20.5g, fat 19.9g, equivalent as salt 0.4g

rocky road cheesecake

serves 12 / prep time 25 minutes / setting time 2–3 hours

150g chocolate chip cookies, crushed
25g desiccated coconut
15g butter, melted
45g crunchy peanut butter
400g Philadelphia, softened
50g caster sugar
200g milk chocolate, melted
50ml double cream
3 rounded tsp powdered gelatine
100g red glacé cherries, roughly chopped
150g marshmallows, halved

LINE the base of a 22cm springform cake tin. Combine the biscuit crumbs, coconut, butter and peanut butter. Press the crumb mixture into the base of the prepared tin.

BEAT the Philly and caster sugar until smooth. Stir in the melted chocolate and cream.

DISSOLVE the gelatine in 125ml of water, over a pan of hot water. Stir the gelatine into the chocolate mixture and fold in the glacé cherries and marshmallows. Pour the mixture over the prepared crust and chill for 2–3 hours until set.

tip To save a little time use glacé cherry halves and mini marshmallows.

Per serving: energy 375kcal, protein 6.1g, carbohydrate 39.7g, fat 22.5g, equivalent as salt 0.5g

fruity frozen cheesecake

serves 10 / prep time 20 minutes / freezing time 2–3 hours

150g low-fat digestive
    biscuits, crushed
50g butter or soft
    margarine, melted
200g Philadelphia, softened
200g caster sugar
250ml raspberry juice
150g fresh or frozen raspberries
200ml whipping cream,
    lightly whipped

LINE the base of a 20cm springform cake tin. Combine the biscuit crumbs and butter and press into the base of the prepared tin. Chill.

BEAT the Philly and sugar together until smooth. Gently stir in the raspberry juice, raspberries and whipped cream. Spoon into the prepared base.

FREEZE for 2–3 hours or until firm. Remove from the freezer about 15 minutes before serving to soften slightly.

tip If you can't find raspberry juice use raspberry and cranberry or a raspberry and apple mix. Darker-coloured juices may alter the colour of the cheesecake mixture, giving a lovely pale pink hue.

Per serving: energy 328kcal, protein 2.9g, carbohydrate 36.7g, fat 19.4g, equivalent as salt 0.5g

honey and ginger cheesecake

serves 10 / prep time 20 minutes / setting time 2–3 hours

50g butter or soft margarine,
    melted
150g ginger biscuits, crushed
225g Philadelphia Light
150ml natural yoghurt
4 tbsp clear honey
3 rounded tsp powdered gelatine
125ml whipping cream, lightly
    whipped

STIR the melted butter into the crushed biscuits. Press the mixture firmly into a lined, loose-bottomed 20cm cake tin and chill until required.

BEAT the Philly, yoghurt and honey together until smooth. Dissolve the gelatine in 3 tablespoons of water, over a pan of hot water. Stir the gelatine and whipped cream into the Philly mixture.

SPOON the mixture over the prepared base and chill for 2–3 hours until set.

tip To crush the biscuits pop them in a re-sealable bag and bash with a rolling pin. Alternatively, whizz them in a food processor until crushed.

Per serving: energy 228kcal, protein 4.5g, carbohydrate 22.0g, fat 14.1g, equivalent as salt 0.5g

cool and creamy cheesecake

serves 10 / prep time 30 minutes / setting time 3–4 hours

75g butter or soft margarine
200g digestive biscuits, crushed
450g Philadelphia Light, softened
100ml semi-skimmed milk
150g caster sugar
zest and juice of 1 lemon
1 × 11g sachet of gelatine
100ml double cream, lightly
    whipped
fresh fruits, to decorate

MELT the butter and mix with the crushed biscuit crumbs. Press into the base of a lined 20cm springform cake tin and chill.

BEAT the Philly until soft and smooth. Add the milk, sugar, lemon zest and juice. Mix thoroughly.

DISSOLVE the gelatine in 3 tablespoons of water, over a pan of hot water. Add to the Philly mixture and then fold in the cream. Pour onto the crumb base and chill in the fridge for 3–4 hours until set.

JUST before serving remove the cheesecake from the tin and decorate with fresh fruit (e.g. figs, nectarines, blackberries and redcurrants).

tip For an extra-fruity version, replace the lemon juice and milk with 250g mashed or puréed soft fruit (e.g. raspberries or strawberries) and add to the Philly with the sugar.

Per serving: energy 353kcal, protein 6.5g, carbohydrate 31.8g, fat 23.1g, equivalent as salt 0.8g

white chocolate and raspberry cheesecake

serves 10 / prep time 30 minutes / setting time 3 hours

200g digestive biscuits, crushed
50g butter, melted
400g Philadelphia, softened
150g caster sugar
1 tsp grated lemon zest
1 × 11g sachet of gelatine
200g white chocolate, melted
200ml whipping cream, lightly
　　whipped
150g frozen raspberries
　　(do not defrost)

To decorate:
200g fresh raspberries and
　　icing sugar

LINE the base of a 20cm springform cake tin. Combine the biscuit crumbs and butter and press into the base of the prepared tin.

BEAT the Philly, sugar and zest using an electric mixer until smooth. Dissolve the gelatine in 50ml of water, over a pan of hot water. Stir in the gelatine mixture and the melted chocolate until smooth, then fold in the cream and frozen raspberries.

POUR the filling into the prepared base and refrigerate for 3 hours or until set. Decorate with raspberries and dust with icing sugar to serve.

tip Fresh raspberries can be used in place of frozen in the cheesecake but use 2 x 11g sachets of gelatine to ensure the cheesecake sets.

Per serving: energy 485kcal, protein 6.6g, carbohydrate 45.5g, fat 32.1g, equivalent as salt 0.8g

orchard pear cheesecake

serves 10 / prep time 20 minutes / setting time 2 – 3 hours

75g butter or soft margarine,
  melted
150g sweet oaty biscuits, crushed
25g rolled oats
2 × 410g cans pear halves, in juice
50g caster sugar
grated zest and juice of ½ lemon
300g Philadelphia Light
3 rounded tsp powdered gelatine
250g fresh chilled custard

LINE the base of a 20cm springform cake tin. Stir the melted butter into the crushed biscuits and oats. Spoon into the base of the tin, press down well and chill until required.

DRAIN and slice the pear halves, reserving the juice. Arrange the pears on the chilled base, reserving some to decorate. Whisk the caster sugar, lemon zest, juice and 2 tablespoons pear juice into the Philly. Dissolve the gelatine in 3 tablespoons of water, over a pan of hot water. Stir the custard and gelatine into the Philly mixture.

SPOON the cheese mixture over the prepared base and pears. Chill for 2–3 hours or until set. Decorate with the reserved pear halves and keep chilled until ready to serve.

tip For an extra-special decoration, drizzle melted dark chocolate over the top of the cheesecake or decorate with flakes of dark chocolate.

Per serving: energy 245kcal, protein 5.4g, carbohydrate 25.5g, fat 13.8g, equivalent as salt 0.6g

index

The symbol (V) indicates where a recipe is suitable for vegetarians

The symbol (V) indicates where a recipe is suitable for vegetarians

acknowledgements

The Philadelphia team would like to thank
everyone who has helped create this book.

Recipe Development and Testing Team
Kraft Home Economist, Emma Warner, with
support from Valerie Hemming and Wendy Strang.

Photography
Will Heap, Photographer and Sarah Tildesley,
Food Stylist.

Marketing Team
Victoria Milner and Carly Jackson.

Thanks also go to:
The team at Ebury Press for their support and
guidance and the Law, Regulatory & Corporate
Affairs team for their enthusiasm and commitment
throughout the project.